IMAGES
of America

ARCADIA

IMAGES

of America

ARCADIA

Arcadia Historical Society

ARCADIA
PUBLISHING

Copyright © 2008 by Arcadia Historical Society
ISBN 978-1-5316-3726-2

Published by Arcadia Publishing
Charleston SC, Chicago IL, Portsmouth NH, San Francisco CA

Library of Congress Catalog Card Number: 2007939180

For all general information contact Arcadia Publishing at:
Telephone 843-853-2070
Fax 843-853-0044
E-mail sales@arcadiapublishing.com
For customer service and orders:
Toll-Free 1-888-313-2665

Visit us on the Internet at www.arcadiapublishing.com

*This book is dedicated to the 166 founding and charter members
of the Arcadia Historical Society and the Woman's Club of Arcadia,
whose foresight and initiative made the society possible.*

CONTENTS

ACKNOWLEDGMENTS

The Arcadia Historical Society would like to thank the following people and organizations, without which this project would never have been possible.

The Arcadia Public Library provided authoritative source material and early photographs. Janet Sporleder, director of Library and Museum Services, and Carolyn Garner-Reagan, Library Services manager, could not have been more helpful and encouraging. Reference librarian Yvonne Ng spent countless hours finding and scanning images.

The Ruth and Charles Gilb Arcadia Historical Museum made its wonderful collections available to us. Special thanks go to curator Alycia Wood and educational coordinator Hwee-Ching Sinclair for their research abilities and for putting up with us. Museum volunteers, including Abraham Ho and Lindsey Sun, were extremely helpful.

Several individuals generously allowed us to use their original photographs and the stories behind them: Jean Parrille, Faye Nouhi, Jerry and Doris Selmer, Roberta Ramsell, Teri Weeks, Barbara and Gary Kovacic, and Tatsushi Nakamura. Valuable reference material came from published material and documents. We wish to thank Sandy Snider for her books, *Arboretum Album* and *Arcadia: Where Ranch and City Meet*, and for sharing information about Anoakia. She also helped proof our first chapter and provided valuable insights into the Baldwin years.

This book would not exist without the dedicated efforts of the four authors who pooled their time and talents: Carol Libby, Jack McCrea, Scott Hettrick, and Jena Ball. Carol was the inspiration and guiding light behind this project. Her knowledge of Arcadia history is truly remarkable, and her unwavering dedication kept the project on track. Jena, Jack, and Scott each authored chapters of the book, and Jena oversaw the final edits.

INTRODUCTION

The city of Arcadia lies on land that was once part of the San Gabriel Mission's enormous land holdings. When Spanish rule gave way to the Independent Republic of Mexico in 1821, much of the acreage belonging to the missions became public land. In 1839, Hugo Reid, a Scotsman who became a Mexican citizen, petitioned the Los Angeles Ayuntamiento (council) for title to the three square leagues (13,319 acres) that would become Santa Anita Rancho. This large tract extended from San Gabriel in the south to the Sierra Madre mountain range in the north. Reid was granted full title to the land in 1845.

Over the next 30 years, Santa Anita Rancho changed ownership five times. In 1875, the man whose energy and vision would shape the rancho's future arrived on the scene: Elias Jackson "Lucky" Baldwin, an entrepreneur whose fortunes had been made in the mining industry. Baldwin was impressed by the beauty and fertility of the land and purchased 8,000 acres for $200,000.

Baldwin turned his 8,000 acres into a profitable working ranch that became famous for its produce, livestock, and stable of pampered Thoroughbred racehorses. Later, after selling portions of the rancho to Nathaniel Carter and William Monroe (the developers of Sierra Madre and Monrovia respectively), Baldwin became interested in forming a city of his own. Incorporated in 1903, after some heated debate about how Baldwin planned to run it, Arcadia had its borders as Baldwin's private property on the west (what is now the Los Angeles County Arboretum and Botanic Garden) and the town of Monrovia to the east. As Arcadia's first mayor, Baldwin used his famed Oakwood Hotel as the seat of the new government.

Baldwin's big plans included a new school and a "paper that can talk back." Law and order were maintained by a marshal and deputies along with a court and jail facilities. To finance these improvements, an ordinance requiring businesses to purchase $40 liquor licenses was passed. Arcadia's other source of income was the tourist trade, which included revenue from Baldwin's Santa Anita Racetrack. Opened in 1907, on the site of what is currently Los Angeles County's Arcadia Park, the track was the realization of one of Baldwin's biggest dreams. That same year, Arcadia's first grammar school was built at First Avenue and California Street.

The character of Arcadia began to change dramatically when Baldwin died in 1909 and California declared horse racing illegal. The city grew, expanding water and electricity services and postal distribution. In 1912, residents demanded that liquor sales be abolished. A fire department was established after two disastrous blazes destroyed Baldwin's Oakwood Hotel and the racetrack's grandstand. Streets were also lighted, graded, and oiled.

The World War I era saw the site of the original Santa Anita Racetrack become Ross Field, the home of an army balloon training school. The land was originally owned by Anita Baldwin, Lucky's daughter, who sold it to Los Angeles County, which in turn deeded it to the War Department.

The 1920s were marked by economic prosperity and rapid development. Large tracts of land were allocated for 1-acre homesites. By then, Arcadia was the poultry capital of Southern California, supplying thousands of eggs a day to grocers and residents throughout Los Angeles County. But in 1929, the stock market crashed and the subsequent Depression hit Arcadia hard. Business failures, unemployment, and political turmoil were common. Despite the need for frugality, two large projects were completed during the 1930s—Santa Anita Park in 1934 and the largest real estate transaction in Arcadia's history in 1936.

The park was built on 400 acres of original ranch land and would eventually be used as a Japanese relocation center, an army ordnance training center, and a holding area for prisoners of war during World War II. The land transaction involved 1,300 acres of the remaining Baldwin Ranch, which were sold by Anita Baldwin to Harry Chandler, publisher of the *Los Angeles Times*. Chandler established Rancho Santa Anita, Inc., as a real estate syndicate.

The 1940s saw the establishment of Los Angeles County's arboretum on acreage purchased for $320,000 by the State of California and Los Angeles County. Operated by the Los Angeles Arboretum Foundation and the county Parks and Recreation Department, it serves as a botanical and horticultural center. Historical landmarks on the property include Baldwin's Queen Anne Cottage and Coach Barn, the Santa Anita Depot, and the Hugo Reid Adobe. The population explosion of the 1950s and 1960s demanded new schools, which were built to accommodate the student population. The 1980s brought additional changes as Arcadia welcomed new faces, voices, and cultures to its already eclectic mix of citizens.

Today Arcadia calls itself a "Community of Homes" and is known for its fine schools, outstanding library services, community-oriented police and fire departments, and world-class Methodist Hospital. The population is up from 360 in 1903 to around 53,000, more than fulfilling the dreams of its ambitious founder.

ARCADIA HISTORICAL SOCIETY

The Woman's Club of Arcadia recognized the value of the city's past, organizing on November 16, 1952, the Arcadia Historical Society. Dewey E. Nelson, the historical curator from the Los Angeles State and County Arboretum, suggested forming the society, and Mrs. Nancy Hutton, the chairwoman of the Woman's Club of Arcadia, spearheaded the organization. Members worked out of the Arcadia High School cafeteria or the arboretum until 1954, when William Parker Lyon Jr. of the Pony Express Museum donated an old Indian trading post, which was moved to the park. The society refurbished Lucky Baldwin's Queen Anne Cottage and restored and relocated the Santa Anita Depot in 1970 and the Hugo Reid Statue in 2003. The society's most recent project is to fulfill an original goal to place educational markers at historic sites throughout the community.

One

THE BALDWIN RANCH

From its birth in 1903, Arcadia has had its share of memorable characters, including card sharks, movie moguls, and a poultry-raising prince. But it was Arcadia's colorful founder, Elias Jackson Baldwin, with his knack for accumulating wealth, who defined and shaped Arcadia's personality.

Born in Hamilton County, Ohio, on April 3, 1828, Elias Jackson (E. J.) Baldwin was taught to love the land and appreciate the value of money. That he had learned his lessons well became apparent when, at the age of 12, he talked his father into letting him take 200 hogs to market and keep a portion of the proceeds. With his share of the profits, Elias purchased gifts, a shotgun, and a horse with resale potential. This ability to see the potential in everything from livestock to businesses made Baldwin a multimillionaire and earned him the nickname "Lucky Baldwin."

Lucky Baldwin found the California Gold Rush irresistible. In 1853, he sold his successful business in Wisconsin and traveled with his family to San Francisco. There he began amassing the first of many fortunes by investing in real estate and Comstock mining shares. While investigating the rumor of gold in Southern California in 1875, Baldwin fell in love with Santa Anita Rancho. "Nothing will make me happy but to own it," Baldwin exclaimed.

Within weeks, Baldwin acquired the rancho and began turning it into a profitable paradise. Despite financial and personal tumult, Baldwin made the ranch flourish. Heralded as one of the most beautiful places on earth, it was a successful working ranch, producing livestock, vegetables, wines, and Thoroughbreds. In 1903, Baldwin announced plans to incorporate the ranch portion known as Arcadia. Elections were held, and in July 1903, the city of Arcadia became a reality. By the time of his death in 1909, Baldwin had transformed his ranch into a thriving city full of excitement, charm, and economic opportunity.

BALDWIN IN 1875, AGE 47. At the time this photograph was taken, Elias Jackson (E. J.) Baldwin was already a famous and wealthy man. He became a multimillionaire through a variety of business ventures, including stock transactions and real estate. The same year he was elected president of the Pacific Stock Exchange, the Baldwin Hotel was nearing completion in San Francisco. He purchased three large ranchos in Southern California (Santa Anita, La Cienega, and San Francisquito) and acquired a string of Kentucky-bred Thoroughbreds. (Courtesy Arcadia Public Library.)

SANTA ANITA CANYON. Baldwin was on his way to investigate a possible mining venture in the San Bernardino Mountains when he passed through Santa Anita Rancho in the San Gabriel Valley. Legend has it that he got down from his horse, sifted some soil through his fingers, and exclaimed, "This can grow anything. It is paradise. I must have this land." (Courtesy Arcadia Public Library.)

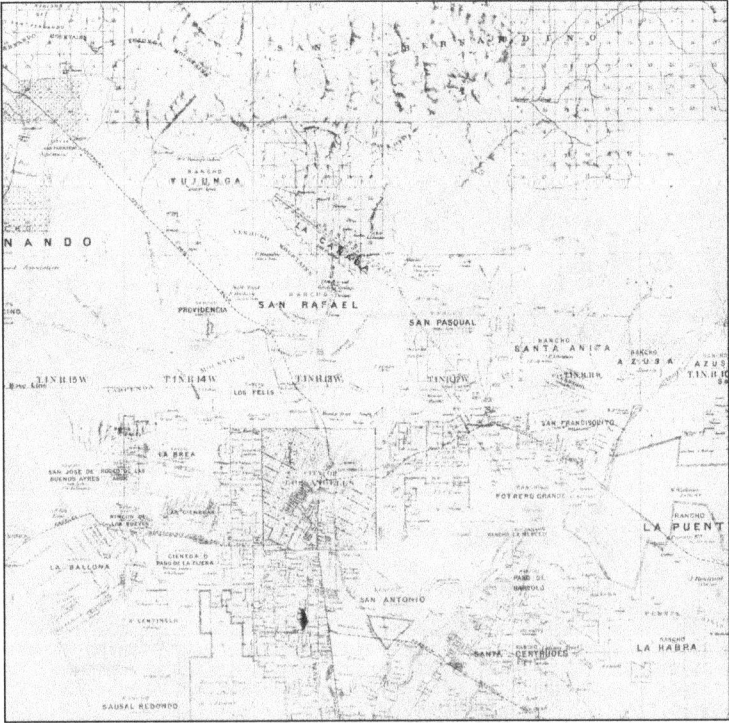

SANTA ANITA RANCHO MAP. E. J. Baldwin purchased the 8,000-acre Santa Anita Rancho and water rights to the Santa Anita Canyon from Harris Newmark for $200,000 in the spring of 1875. The water rights were crucial to productive farmland. Baldwin spared no expense to bring the canyon's streams to his land. He put a large crew to work digging the ditches to transport the water to his fields. (Courtesy Arcadia Public Library.)

CALIFORNIA LIVE OAK. Baldwin revered the California oak trees on his property. No one was allowed to cut them down, not even for firewood. He planted trees along the sides of all the streets in his township and used imported trees from throughout the world to decorate his rancho. These included elms, maples, acacias, cypress, silk oak, a grove of palms, and a stand of Monterey pines. (Courtesy Arcadia Public Library.)

SHEEP GRAZING IN THE FOOTHILLS. Large herds of sheep were pastured in the foothills and tended by Basque herders. Hundreds of horses and mules, along with thousands of cattle, grazed on the flatlands below. Baldwin built a dairy on the western boundary of the rancho and outfitted it with the most up-to-date equipment available. His herd consisted of Jerseys and Holsteins, as well as imported breeds. (Courtesy Arcadia Public Library.)

RANCHO ORCHARDS. By 1891, five hundred acres of Santa Anita Rancho were devoted to citrus groves containing 16,000 orange and lemon trees. Proud of the fact that he was beholden to no one, Baldwin produced, packed, and marketed his fruit under his own label. A 75-acre orchard could produce 80,000 boxes of oranges, netting him the tidy sum of $120,000. (Courtesy Huntington Library Collection.)

PRIZE-WINNING WINES AND BRANDIES. Baldwin's vineyards grew the grapes used by his winery to produce fine wines and brandies. Both were acclaimed by connoisseurs in the United States and Europe. Orange champagne was his winery's specialty. One price list offered old port, 20 years old, $10; grape brandy, 20 years old, $20; orange brandy, 15 years old, $15; and Burgundy, 7 years old, $7.50 per case. (Courtesy Arcadia Public Library.)

THE RANCHO TRAINING TRACK. E. J. Baldwin was a consummate horseman who maintained a stable of Thoroughbreds and a mile-long training track. Baldwin's first Thoroughbreds, purchased in 1874, were Grinstead and Rutherford. By 1875, he had acquired breeding mares. Baldwin pioneered breeding and training Thoroughbreds in California, racing his horses successfully across the country. Horses to be raced in the east were transported in his two Pullman Palace horse cars named the "Arcadia" and the "Santa Anita." (Courtesy Arcadia Public Library.)

BALDWIN'S ADOBE. Baldwin's residence was an updated and improved version of Hugo Reid's original adobe and wood home. It had eight rooms, including a dining room, kitchen, and bedrooms. There was also a room for servants and a large porch with Victorian posts and trellises. Baldwin called his home the "Adobe." (Courtesy Arcadia Public Library.)

COACH BARN, C. 1880. The coach barn housed 14 different carriages for Baldwin's personal use. The barn was constructed of redwood and paneled with alternating slats of redwood and Port Orford cedar. Living quarters were located on the upper floor. Other nearby buildings included stables, cottages for employees and their families, and a ranch store. (Courtesy Huntington Library Collection.)

QUEEN ANNE COTTAGE, C. 1890. Completed in 1886, this lovely Victorian home was referred to as "Baldwin's Belvedere" or "Baldwin's Casino." The architect was Albert A. Bennett, designer of the California Capitol Building dome and the governor's mansion in Sacramento. Beautiful stained-glass windows, marble steps and porches, and filigreed porticos made this an ideal setting for Baldwin to entertain his many guests. (Courtesy Arcadia Public Library.)

SANTA ANITA RANCH STORE. Baldwin maintained a general store on his ranch that was patronized by the residents of Sierra Madre as well as ranch hands and their families, who received credit since their wages were frequently in arrears. Store-bought goods were delivered free of charge. Advertisements indicate that the store carried hosiery, notions, groceries, liquors, clothing, carpets, wines, and lumber. (Courtesy Arcadia Public Library.)

15

SANTA ANITA DEPOT, C. 1890. Baldwin began building the two-story Santa Anita Depot after negotiating a right-of-way deed with the Santa Fe Railroad. Its trains were required to stop at Santa Anita Rancho. The depot was constructed of bricks from the brickyard on Baldwin's ranch and completed in 1890. The second floor provided living quarters for the depot's agent. Baldwin tested his agreement with Santa Fe by asking to purchase a ticket to his ranch on his way home from Big Bear. When the ticket agent told him trains didn't stop at the ranch, Baldwin asked for a blank telegram form, on which he wrote, "Put 200 men to work tearing up Santa Fe tracks throughout my ranch." When the agent read the telegram and realized who he was, Baldwin got his ticket. (Courtesy Arcadia Public Library.)

THE OAKWOOD HOTEL. In 1887, Baldwin completed the Oakwood Hotel in the center of what would be the township of Arcadia. The two-story, brick building was across from the train depot. There were 35 rooms, each with a fireplace and hot and cold running water. The Oakwood also had a restaurant, post office, and telephone and telegraph services. Trains from both the Santa Fe and Southern Pacific Railroads passed in front of the hotel. An advertisement for the Oakwood mentioned that the travel time from Los Angeles to Santa Anita was only 45 minutes. (Courtesy Arcadia Public Library.)

BANK OVERDRAFT LETTER.
Though a millionaire, Lucky
Baldwin was often in debt and
regularly sued by his creditors
for failure to pay his bills or
meet his financial obligations.
What cash he did have, Baldwin
put back into investments.
He was quoted as saying, "If
anyone wants anything out of
me, they'll have to sue. I want
a reputation of being hard
to collect from." (Courtesy
Arcadia Historical Society.)

17

PEAFOWL IMPORTED FROM INDIA. Lucky Baldwin first encountered peafowl in India during the world tour he took in 1867. Before leaving on his tour, Baldwin placed shares of stock in a safe and instructed his broker to sell them when they reached their purchase price. When Baldwin returned to San Francisco two years later, he found that the broker had been unable to sell the stock because Baldwin had forgotten to give him the key to the safe. Luckily for Baldwin, the stock's value had increased by more than 15 times its purchase price. The press had a field day with the story, christening him "Lucky Baldwin," a nickname that stuck. Baldwin subsequently imported some of the peafowl in the 1880s. (Courtesy Arcadia Historical Society.)

A RANCH ATTRACTION—LOG CABIN. Baldwin valued this log cabin as a reminder of the history of Santa Anita Rancho. Perhaps it also reminded him of his boyhood days in Ohio and Indiana or of the days of the Comstock Lode. The cabin was used as an apiary and was a popular attraction for tourists who came to visit. (Courtesy Arcadia Public Library.)

THE MISSING BELL. For many years, the San Gabriel Mission bell occupied a prominent place on Baldwin's ranch. How Baldwin obtained the bell is uncertain. One story says that an earthquake caused the bell to fall from its tower and Baldwin recovered it; another claims he purchased it. Either way, the bell remained on the ranch until the 1920s, when his daughter Anita returned it to the mission. (Courtesy Arcadia Public Library.)

A CACTUS SPECIMEN, C. 1890. Baldwin was often asked what he raised on his ranch. "Everything in the world but the mortgage," he would reply. This old postcard shows one of Baldwin's prized cactus plants. Other favorites included calla lilies, roses, and a weeping willow planted by the lake. The willow was said to have come from a cutting taken from a willow growing close to Napoleon's tomb. (Courtesy Arcadia Historical Society.)

Entrance to E. J. (Lucky) Baldwin's Private Grounds, Baldwin's Ranch, Cal.

ENTRANCE TO BALDWIN'S PRIVATE GROUNDS. Little expense was spared on Baldwin's landscaping projects. Baldwin himself is said to have directed the placement of each and every plant. A wall of evergreen hedges, combined with semitropical plants, created a stunning entrance to his private grounds. The use of natural materials and rare plants was a Baldwin trademark. (Courtesy Arcadia Historical Society.)

BALDWIN FAMILY PORTRAIT—
FOUR GENERATIONS. In this
photograph, Baldwin is surrounded
by his daughter Clara, his
granddaughter Rosebudd Doble,
with her son Joe Mullender.
Rosebudd's father was Budd Doble,
a world-famous trotting horse
driver. Not pictured is Clara's son
Albert from a second marriage
to Albert Snyder. (Courtesy
Arcadia Public Library.)

BALDWIN FAMILY
PORTRAIT—THREE
GENERATIONS. This
family portrait shows
Baldwin seated
with his daughter
Anita and her two
children—Dextra
and Baldwin. When
Anita divorced her
children's father, Hull
McClaughry, she and
the children took
her maiden name.
Dextra comes from
the name Dexter,
the maiden name
of Anita's mother.
(Courtesy Arcadia
Public Library.)

BALDWIN'S ESTATE IS SETTLED.
Lucky Baldwin died in 1909 at the age of 81, and it took four years to settle his estate. Daughters Clara and Anita received the bulk of the estate. When the final settlement was reached in 1913, they received about $20 million between them. (Courtesy Arcadia Public Library.)

CHAIN OF TITLE.
This document shows the owners of Santa Anita Rancho in chronological order. Several figured prominently in California's growth and development, including Hugo Reid, William Wolfskill, and E. J. Baldwin. Each time the rancho was sold, it decreased in size. Reid was granted 13,000 acres; Baldwin purchased 8,000; and Chandler was only able to obtain 1,300. (Courtesy Arcadia Public Library.)

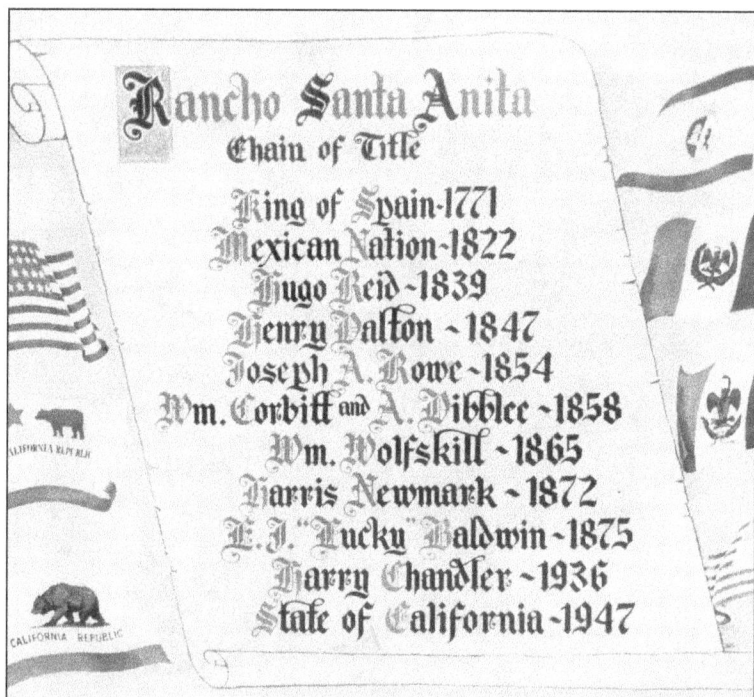

Rancho Santa Anita
Chain of Title

King of Spain -1771
Mexican Nation -1822
Hugo Reid -1839
Henry Dalton -1847
Joseph A. Rowe -1854
Wm. Corbitt and A. Dibblee -1858
Wm. Wolfskill -1865
Harris Newmark -1872
E. J. "Lucky" Baldwin -1875
Harry Chandler -1936
State of California -1947

Two

A City is Born

The start of the 20th century marked the beginning of a three-decade growth spurt in Southern California. The slow-paced, agrarian lifestyle of the haciendas was giving way to the hustle and bustle of urban life as Los Angeles, Pasadena, and Monrovia began to grow into thriving cities.

Inevitably, the excitement and energy that accompanied this shift captured the attention of Elias Jackson "Lucky" Baldwin. Though Baldwin's ranch was thriving, he sensed new and bigger opportunities were developing. In March 1903, he petitioned to incorporate the township of Arcadia into a city. Located on Baldwin's ranch, the town of 360 people had little to recommend it other than scenic beauty. Baldwin's plan was to clean up the township in preparation for future development. However, Baldwin's detractors feared he would turn Arcadia into, according to a July 28, 1903, *Los Angeles Times* article, "A gambling hell and booze park," and they formed the Anti-Saloon League to oppose him. Despite their best efforts, Baldwin prevailed, carrying all but one of the votes and becoming mayor to boot.

The first order of business was to call a meeting of the board of trustees and set up a committee to create a school for the city. In subsequent meetings, several money-making ordinances were passed, including a $40 liquor license for businesses serving alcohol, fines for damaging trees or leaving horses unhitched for more than five minutes, and a $10 license for peddlers.

Since tourism and entertainment (gambling, alcohol, bowling, boxing, horse and dog racing, and musical comedies) formed the core of Arcadia's economy, the city quickly acquired a reputation for being flamboyant and rowdy. The opening of the Santa Anita Racetrack in December 1907 drew more than 7,000 visitors and did little to dispel this impression. Unfortunately, there was little the average citizen of Arcadia could do to curtail disorderly conduct in the city, and it wasn't until Baldwin's death in 1909 that things began to change. Even then, it took three years and the determined efforts by more civic-minded residents to get the sale of alcohol banned and to establish a library, church, and other community organizations.

ARCADIA'S SANTE FE DEPOT, 1900. This wooden, gingerbread-trim depot served passengers traveling to Arcadia by train. Located on the south side of the tracks and north of the Oakwood Hotel, it featured an open waiting room and baggage area. After train service ended, it was moved to the Los Angeles County Fairgrounds in Pomona in 1969. Arcadia residents Effie and George McCoy are pictured here. (Courtesy Arcadia Public Library.)

THE FIRST BUSINESS BUILDING, C. 1910. This large, two-story building was owned by the McCoy family. Known as the "McCoy Block," it was located in the heart of Arcadia's business district. The building housed a variety of businesses and provided meeting space for clubs and churches. When the Oakwood Hotel burned, the upper floor of the McCoy Block served as city hall. Rent was $5 a month. (Courtesy Arcadia Public Library.)

Arcadia's First School Building, 1903. Donated by Mayor E. J. Baldwin, Arcadia's first school was a packing shed placed on the corner of Santa Anita and Falling Leaf Avenue (now Huntington Drive). Fifty-eight students were enrolled when the school opened its doors in September 1903. One teacher was hired to teach all grades. For many children, it was a long walk to and from school. (Courtesy Arcadia Public Library.)

Arcadia Grammar School, 1908. Baldwin's shed served as Arcadia's schoolhouse for four years. Then lots were purchased on First Avenue at California Street, and a schoolhouse was built for the 1907–1908 school year. With two classrooms in the rear and a library in front, it accommodated 65 pupils and two teachers. Grades one through four were taught together, as were grades five through eight. (Courtesy Arcadia Public Library.)

ATTRACTIONS AT BALDWIN RANCH. Tally-ho carriage rides from Baldwin Ranch to the Oakwood Hotel could be arranged daily. Visitors to the ranch were delighted by the great variety of plants Lucky had acquired. "Grand scenery" and "an Earthly Paradise" were just some of the comments made by guests. The use of boulders to edge pathways, ponds, the lake, and flower beds was a Baldwin tradition. (Courtesy Arcadia Historical Society.)

WHITE CITY SALOON, C. 1907. This popular saloon was reached via a dirt road running west from Santa Anita Avenue and parallel to the railroad tracks. The saloon offered musical comedies and vaudeville acts every evening. Other entertainment included a merry-go-round, hot-air balloon rides, and baseball on Sundays. An advertisement touted perfect cuisine and moderate prices. A fire destroyed the saloon in 1909. (Courtesy Arcadia Public Library.)

BONITA HOTEL OPERATORS, C.
1890. J. Augustin De Lude and his
wife operated the Bonita Hotel for
many years with help from Augustin's
brother Francis and his family. Francis,
his wife, Alphonsine, and their six
children traveled from Sherbrood,
Quebec, to Arcadia by train. The
train made a special stop in front of
the hotel because the group was so
tired. The family stayed four years.
(Courtesy Arcadia Historical Society.)

BONITA HOTEL, 1904. This small, modest hotel and beer garden was owned and operated by
Ben Newman, a city councilman from 1910 to 1911. Tourists who could not afford the prices
at the Oakwood Hotel registered here. The establishment also served as a boardinghouse. As
a councilman in 1911, Newman voted for an ordinance that closed saloons from midnight to
5:00 a.m. (Courtesy Arcadia Public Library.)

OAKWOOD HOTEL AS CITY HALL. Following Arcadia's incorporation in 1903, this hotel served as city hall. In addition to conducting city business (such as council meetings and land sales) there, all kinds of gambling, including roulette wheels and slot machines, was available. Carriage rides and tours of Baldwin Ranch could be arranged at the hotel as well. (Courtesy Arcadia Public Library.)

FIRST STREET ENTRANCE TO FAIRYLAND PARK. BALDWIN'S RANCH

FAIRYLAND PARK AT THE OAKWOOD. When Baldwin renovated the Oakwood Hotel in 1905, he added an outdoor entertainment center and a garden of electrical lights. He hoped to attract tourists by offering good food, fine wine and brandies, and entertainment in the form of vaudeville acts. The renovation cost Baldwin about $10,000. (Courtesy Los Angeles Racing Association Souvenir Booklet.)

BALDWIN'S SANTA ANITA RACETRACK. When Los Angeles outlawed horse racing at Ascot Park, Baldwin quickly negotiated a deal with racing businessmen to build Santa Anita Racetrack. Located on the site of what is currently Los Angeles County's Arcadia Park, the track opened December 7, 1907, with 7,000 fans attending. Baldwin's reaction was to declare, "This is the grandest thing I have ever done, and I am satisfied." (Courtesy Arcadia Public Library.)

BALDWIN'S THOROUGHBREDS. Baldwin bred and raced Thoroughbreds. He had four American Derby winners: Volante in 1885, Silver Cloud in 1886, Emperor of Norfolk in 1888, and Rey El Santa Anita in 1894. Emperor of Norfolk died the night Santa Anita Racetrack opened. Some say that Emperor of Norfolk was the finest California-bred racehorse prior to Swaps, a Kentucky Derby winner and Horse of the Year. (Courtesy Arcadia Public Library.)

A CAR WRECK, C. 1910. In its infancy, "motoring" was a dangerous and uncertain undertaking, especially on Arcadia's rudimentary streets. The city's earliest thoroughfares were dirty and dusty and without signs, speed limits, or lights. Things improved slightly in 1910 when streets were graded and given a layer of oil. This photograph shows Ben Newman's Buick, which was hit by a Santa Fe train. (Courtesy Arcadia Public Library.)

GIANT PUMPKINS TO ADMIRE, 1915. Alcinda "Ma" Payne was proud of her gardens and the vegetables she raised at her home on East Forest Avenue. She took this photograph to prove how successful she was as a gardener. Some images from her photograph collection depicting rural life in early Arcadia were given to the Arcadia Historical Society. (Courtesy Arcadia Historical Society.)

THE FIRST AVIATION SHOW, C. 1910. This is a photograph of Louis Paulman flying his Farman biplane on its return trip to Aviation Park. Paulman set an air distance record by flying from Dominguez Hills to Arcadia. There he circled Baldwin Ranch before heading home. He also set an altitude record of 4,165 feet on January 12, 1910. (Courtesy Huntington Library Collection.)

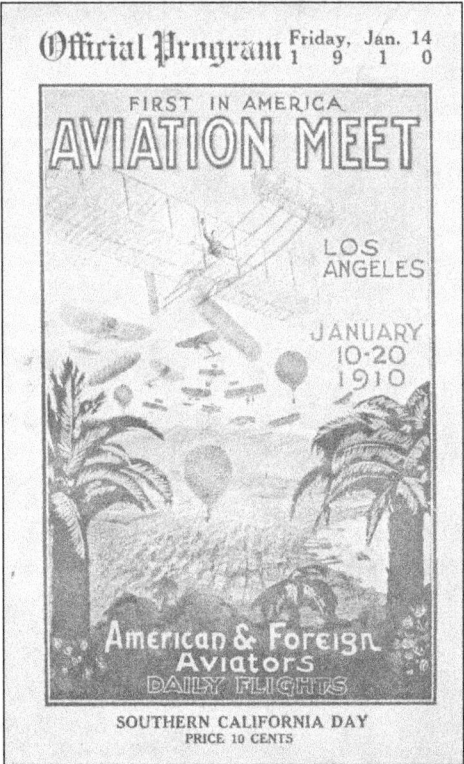

OFFICIAL PROGRAM: AVIATION MEET, 1910. The "First in America" Aviation Meet was held in Los Angeles in January 1910. Prizes were awarded for speed, endurance, the highest altitude attained carrying passengers, the slowest and fastest flights, and the most skillful landing in a specific spot. "Aeroplanes" and dirigible airships also participated for prizes and records at the meet. (Courtesy Arcadia Historical Society.)

BURNELL ESTATE. This mansion, set on 7 acres of land, was purchased by George Edwin Burnell in 1915 from Charles Winship. It is believed that Winship won the property from Lucky Baldwin. The 14-bedroom, nine-bath mansion was built of hand-hewed redwood. Burnell, a well-known and respected philosopher, established a school to advance his ideas on the estate. The mansion was demolished in 1961. (Courtesy Arcadia Historical Society.)

CLARA BALDWIN'S HOME, CANARY COTTAGE. This home was purchased by Clara and her fourth husband, Harold Stocker, in 1907. Stocker was an opera singer who used the stage name "Stuart Harold." Clara died at the age of 81, leaving an endowment fund to be used to build a home for aged women. In later years, the home was referred to as "Twin Oaks." (Courtesy Arcadia Public Library.)

UNRUH HOME. The first private home built in Arcadia belonged to Hiram Unruh. A nephew of Baldwin's first wife, Unruh managed Baldwin's hotel in San Francisco until 1881. Subsequently, he was Baldwin's ranch manager, business associate, and the executor of the Baldwin estate. Unruh was also one of Arcadia's early councilmen and the city's second mayor. Thanks to Unruh, Baldwin never worried about finances. (Courtesy Arcadia Public Library.)

PERKINS HOME, C. 1919. This house is typical of the architectural style found in Arcadia in the early 1900s. It was built on Lemon Avenue by Albert Perkins. Later, in the 1920s, he built a larger home on West Huntington Drive. In 1939, amid political turmoil, Albert became a city councilman and served as mayor from 1940 to 1944. (Courtesy Arcadia Historical Society.)

Grand Ball

Given by

Co-Operative Arcadians

Saturday Eve., December 19, 1914

At

Odd Fellow's Hall

Monrovia

COOPERATIVE ARCADIANS PROGRAM, 1914. In 1912, a group of Arcadia women formed an organization called Cooperative Arcadians. Their purpose was to generate interest in civic improvement and advertise the city by entering a float in the Pasadena Tournament of Roses Parade. Subsequent projects included cleaning up the city park and installing a drinking fountain on Santa Anita Avenue. (Courtesy Arcadia Historical Society.)

ANITA'S 1915 ROSE PARADE ENTRY. This float, entitled "Dove of Peace," was entered by Anita Baldwin McClaughry in the Pasadena Tournament of Roses Parade. The bird, entirely covered in lilies of the valley, hothouse roses, and sprays of maidenhair fern, was 26 feet long and had an 11-foot wingspan. Anita's entry in the 1914 parade (the 25th annual parade) was a huge white peacock. (Courtesy Arcadia Public Library.)

34

SEAQUIST DRUGSTORE, C. 1914. Oscar Seaquist was the first pharmacist to open a drugstore in Arcadia. The store was located on the east side of First Avenue between Santa Clara and St. Joseph Streets. Other early businesses, located across the street from the drugstore, included the McCoy Building, the telephone office, post office, and the Bachert Notions store. (Courtesy Arcadia Public Library.)

MCLEAN'S GARAGE, C. 1919. This photograph depicts the interior of McLean's Garage located at 808 South Santa Anita Avenue, across the road from the army's Ross Field. The building was made of corrugated metal. C. A. McLean is the person wearing the hat. The name of his helper is not known. (Courtesy Arcadia Public Library.)

TROOPS ON THE ROAD, 1918. Arcadians were disturbed by the news that a balloon training center was opening in town. The city was experiencing a water shortage and had no sewer system and only limited police and fire protection. The number of troops was expected to exceed the city's population by two to one. Fortunately, the men were highly disciplined and behaved impeccably throughout the war. (Courtesy Arcadia Historical Society.)

AN EARLY "FILLING STATION." This small filling (gas) station was located on Santa Anita Avenue (also known as "Double Drive") near Lucille Street, across from Ross Field. Eucalyptus trees were planted along both sides of the divided, two-way thoroughfare. Note the classic gas pumps by the curb. (Courtesy Arcadia Public Library.)

ARCADIA DEPOT AND SECTION FOREMAN. Al Ray, a section foreman for the Santa Fe Railroad, is depicted sitting with his legs crossed, looking east. His wife, wearing a Dunkard bonnet, is seated in the buggy. The station was located on Santa Fe's main line. One train, consisting of freight cars and a passenger day coach, arrived every day but Sunday, bringing passengers and the mail. (Courtesy Arcadia Public Library.)

JOHN OTT, CITY MARSHAL, c. 1914. John ("Jack") Ott was Arcadia's city marshal from May to December 1914. He is pictured here on horseback wearing his uniform. Ott family members were active in civic affairs throughout Arcadia's early years. Ott's son Don became Arcadia's chief of police in 1935. (Courtesy Arcadia Public Library.)

ARCADIA'S FIRST CITY HALL. After fire destroyed the Oakwood Hotel in 1911, Arcadia's city offices were without a permanent home. Eventually it became apparent that a city hall would have to be built. Lots were purchased on the northwest corner of Huntington Drive and First Avenue, and an attractive Colonial-style building was constructed at a cost of $18,000. The dedication of the new city hall was held on July 1918. (Courtesy Arcadia Historical Society.)

ARCADIA GRAMMAR SCHOOL. By 1919, additional space was needed to accommodate Arcadia's schoolchildren. That same year, construction of a new schoolhouse began. Considered by the May 7, 1921, Arcadia Journal as "one of the finest examples of school architecture in the state," it had eight classrooms, a library, an assembly hall, and a swimming pool. It served 209 students for two years before more classrooms were added in 1922. (Courtesy Arcadia Historical Society.)

Three

ANOAKIA

Of the many and controversial choices made by Lucky Baldwin, the decision to bequeath half his assets to his daughter Anita was one of the wisest. Born in 1876 to Baldwin and his third wife, Jennie Dexter, Anita was a sensitive child who loved music. Though shy and retiring, she inherited her father's love of animals and head for business—qualities that served her well when she came into her inheritance in 1913.

Under the terms of Baldwin's will, Anita and her sister Clara received a settlement valued at $20 million. Anita promptly leased Clara's half-interest in their property and converted Santa Anita Ranch into a stock-raising business called Anoakia Stock and Breeding Farm. There she focused on breeding and showing livestock and purebred horses.

Second on Anita's agenda was the construction of her extraordinary home—Anoakia. The word "anoakia" was Anita's, devised by combining the first two letters of her name with the word "oak" (as in oak tree) and adding "ia" for euphony. Anoakia, Anita said, meant "where no harm shall befall," and she spared no expense to make it a sanctuary for herself.

Set amid 19 landscaped acres, Anoakia was built on a grand scale at a cost of over $250,000. The main building consisted of three stories and 50 rooms, with a pool, apiary, bathhouse, tennis courts, aviaries, and kennels scattered across the property. Anita filled Anoakia with modern conveniences, one-of-a-kind artwork by California artists, and elegant, comfortable furnishings.

Over the years, Anita gave generously of her time and resources to a variety of organizations, including the Children's Orthopedic Hospital, the Society for the Prevention of Cruelty to Animals (SPCA), and the Red Star Society. She also helped with the war effort, donating horses to the Army Remount Service, and supported women's and Native American causes.

Eventually, in her later years, Anita grew tired of business and began selling stock and property. This allowed her to indulge her passions for music and travel. The last of her 1,300 acres was sold in July 1936, just three years before her death in 1939 at the age of 66.

ANITA M. BALDWIN (1876–1939). A daughter of E. J. "Lucky" Baldwin and his third wife, Jennie Dexter, Anita was just five years old when her mother died. Born and raised in San Francisco, she was a shy, musically inclined child who inherited her father's love of animals and nature. She married twice and raised two children—Dextra and Baldwin. (Courtesy Arcadia Public Library.)

THE ANOAKIA ESTATE, 1913. Built in 1913 at a cost of over $250,000, this 50-room mansion on 19 acres was located just outside Arcadia's city limits. For protection, the entire estate was walled and guarded. The property included sports facilities for Anita's children (a pool, bathhouse, and tennis courts), plus landscaped gardens, ponds, and hundreds of trees—particularly oaks. (Courtesy Arcadia Public Library.)

ANOAKIA POND. Anita's love of nature was evident throughout the Anoakia estate. Each carefully selected addition was planted where it would thrive and enhance the overall appearance of the garden. In particular, Anita favored the majestic Englemann oaks and sycamores. Sculptures, statues, and objects of art were strategically placed to create an impression of serenity and understated elegance. (Courtesy Arcadia Public Library.)

ANITA FEEDING DEER. Anita was a true animal lover. She served as president of the Los Angeles SPCA in 1921 and was the head of the Red Star Society, which treated and cared for animals wounded in World War I. She also contributed $50,000 in 1919 to benefit Children's Orthopedic Hospital and an additional $50,000 in 1921 to build a new hospital for babies at California Hospital. (Courtesy Arcadia Public Library.)

ANITA'S PRIZED PERCHERON. A respected publication had this to say about Santa Anita Ranch and Anoakia Stock and Breeding Farm: "There is not another fertile spot on the Pacific Coast that is more suitable for raising purebred livestock than this place." Equine, bovine, and swine experts oversaw the care and breeding of purebred horses, Jacks and Jennets, Holstein-Friesian cattle, and Berkshire and Poland-China swine. (Courtesy Arcadia Public Library.)

ANITA IN THE ROSE PARADE. Here Anita is seen in the 1920 Pasadena Tournament of Roses Parade. She is flanked by two of her assistants (both unidentified) as they rode down Colorado Boulevard. In this same year, the idea of building a Rose Bowl stadium was first proposed. (Courtesy Arcadia Public Library.)

ON THE PARADE ROUTE. The year 1920 was the first year float entries in the Pasadena Tournament of Roses Parade were motorized. Only the Hotel Raymond entry was drawn by horses. Shown here is the Santa Anita Ranch entry preceded by uniformed attendants walking with four of Anita's purebred dogs on leashes. (Courtesy Arcadia Historical Society, Bruce Wetmore Collection.)

SANTA ANITA RANCH FLOAT. Anita's entry in the 1920 Pasadena Tournament of Roses Parade featured a red star signifying her involvement in the Red Star Society. This organization treated and cared for animals wounded in World War I. In 1921, Anita was president of the Los Angeles SPCA. (Courtesy Arcadia Historical Society, Bruce Wetmore Collection.)

ANITA'S CHILDREN, C. 1906. Anita's daughter Dextra is pictured standing beside the buggy holding her brother Baldwin. Dextra (born in 1901) was a Southern California debutante, a Marlborough student, and known for spending money lavishly on jewelry, clothes, and furs. She died in 1967. Baldwin became a Southern California developer, yachtsman, and art collector. He also served as secretary of the Pasadena Art Museum. He died in 1970. (Courtesy Arcadia Public Library.)

PORTRAIT OF ANITA, 1917. This portrait of Anita Baldwin shows her at Anoakia with a peacock behind her. The peacock, brought from India by her father, may symbolize her individuality and love of the arts. Anita was a gifted musician who aspired to be a concert pianist until she injured her wrist. It is said that her father often asked her to play for him. (Courtesy Archives of the Pasadena Museum of History.)

Four

Ross Field
The Balloon School

Since its incorporation in 1903, Arcadia has seen a lot of history come and go. One of the most memorable events coincided with the advent of World War I when 1,800 men arrived to convert Lucky Baldwin's former racetrack into a military balloon school. Christened Ross Field after Lt. Cleo Ross (a balloon pilot who lost his life in France), the 185-acre facility was built on land once owned by Anita Baldwin. Anita sold the property to Los Angeles County, which in turn deeded it to the War Department for use in reconnaissance training.

Hydrogen balloons, made of rubberized cotton and filled with highly flammable hydrogen gas, were used to look behind enemy lines and direct military maneuvers on the ground. This was accomplished by sending a trained observer, riding in a basket suspended from the underbelly of the balloon, anywhere from 1,000 to 4,000 feet into the air. Training for these dangerous missions was rigorous as the observer needed to be familiar with artillery operations, signals, maps, and instruments as well as the fundamentals of a Caquot balloon.

Begun in May 1918, Ross Field was up and running in less than four months. Eight training balloons were usually kept in the air from sunup to sundown, and daily trips were made to the summit of Mount Wilson. There, cadets learned the fundamentals of observation and mapping before taking to the skies.

By all accounts, the presence of the balloon school had an immediate and lasting impact on Arcadia. Though they were well disciplined, the presence of so many troops severely taxed the city's infrastructure. Without a sewer system, and in the midst of a drought, Arcadia was hard pressed to meet the increased demand for water. Moreover, its police force was minuscule and the fire department an all-volunteer force. Nevertheless, as is often the case in times of war, everyone worked together to make the best of the situation. By the time the school closed in 1920, Ross Field had contributed significantly to the army's fledgling Air Corps and Arcadia had become an adept and gracious host.

ROSS FIELD, C. 1919. Ross Field was located on the site of Los Angeles County's Arcadia Park. This view looks east with two balloon hangars in the foreground and the Pacific Electric Railway and Southern Pacific Railroad tracks on the left. To the right, running parallel to the line of trees, is Santa Anita Avenue (Double Drive). The rows of buildings in the upper left are barracks. The rest are mostly administrative buildings. The wash in the foreground is just west of today's Arcadia High School on Campus Drive. The dirt oval to the right of the hangars was the site of Lucky Baldwin's original racetrack, which opened in 1907 and closed in 1909. (Courtesy Arcadia Public Library.)

PREPARING TO LAUNCH, C. 1918. Here soldiers at Ross Field are preparing to launch one of their eight reconnaissance balloons. Each balloon carried one or two observers and their equipment in a sturdy, four-by-four-foot wicker basket suspended from its underbelly. The balloons were captive, meaning they were anchored by cables to heavy military trucks (known as Cunninghams) that prevented them from drifting off course. (Courtesy Arcadia Historical Society.)

BALLOON BASKET, C. 1918. Trained observers, riding in baskets beneath their balloons, could see as far as 10 miles behind enemy lines. Their job was to observe and transmit information about the enemy and help direct artillery fire. Observers located enemy guns by the flashes produced when the guns were fired. At the balloon school, new cadets trained for this job by locating mirror flashes. (Courtesy Arcadia Historical Society.)

BALLOONS OVER ARCADIA, C. 1919. These 100-foot, teardrop-shaped balloons were known as Caquots. Named after Lt. Albert Caquot, the French engineer who improved balloon design, they were used as information-gathering tools. However, Caquots could also be dangerous and difficult to control. A 60-man ground crew, composed of riggers, bombers, electricians, and hydrogen experts, was required to maintain each balloon. The hydrogen detail had the riskiest job, as the static electricity in their hair could ignite the highly flammable gas. To prevent this from happening, members of the crew were required to wear skullcaps. In contrast, the bombers were given the task of using smoke bombs to simulate the dust clouds created when an enemy shell hit the ground. In an actual battle, balloons would quickly descend, or the pilot would parachute out, if enemy aircraft approached too close. (Courtesy Arcadia Historical Society.)

FIELD HEADQUARTERS, C. 1918. The first school for training balloon observers was set up in Fort Omaha, Nebraska. However, unfavorable weather conditions forced the Army Air Corps to look for a more suitable location. Arcadia was chosen in May 1918, and Col. W. M. Hensley arrived shortly thereafter to begin setting up the school. By October of that same year, Ross Field was complete. (Courtesy Arcadia Public Library.)

SWIMMING POOL, C. 1918. This pool was originally a reservoir. Anita Baldwin donated it for use by the personnel at Ross Field. Water was regularly drawn off to irrigate fields and replaced by Arcadia's water system. Everyone was required to pass a swimming test before using the pool. If an individual failed the test, swimming lessons were mandatory. (Courtesy Arcadia Public Library.)

ROSS FIELD PHOTOGRAPHERS. Ross Field was the first balloon school to make use of aerial photographs taken from planes. Images were taken of possible enemy targets suggested by the balloon pilots. They were then used to update or change the maps the balloon reconnaissance teams used before their next ascents. Not surprisingly, the large balloons were often targeted by enemy aircraft. (Courtesy Arcadia Historical Society.)

CUNNINGHAM TRUCK, C. 1918. These large, heavy trucks were tethered to balloons by steel cables to keep them from drifting. When it was time for a balloon to be "put to bed," a gasoline-powered winch was used to bring it down from the sky. The old racetrack grandstand initially served as a windbreak for the balloons once they were bedded down for the night. (Courtesy Arcadia Public Library.)

CALISTHENICS, C. 1920. Soldiers in training were assigned two kinds of duties: command (general) and rated (specialty). Command duties included tasks such as playing the bugle, tailoring uniforms, and digging trenches. On a typical day at the front in France, a soldier would work on a balloon team during the day and help move it to a new location at night. (Courtesy Arcadia Public Library.)

ROSS FIELD LOOKING NORTH. The Goodyear Aerospace Corporation of Ohio manufactured nearly 1,000 Caquot balloons for use in the war. Only one, built in 1944 for use in British parachute tests and photography, survived. It has since been restored and is now on display at Wright Patterson Air Force Base in Ohio. (Courtesy Arcadia Historical Society.)

BALLOON SCHOOL STUDENTS, c. 1918. In addition to having a working knowledge of artillery operations, signals, maps, and instruments, balloon observers were expected to learn how to minimize attacks by enemy aircraft and antiaircraft (AA) fire. Because of their size, lack of speed, and flammability, balloons were often the targets of enemy fire, and plane pilots on both sides spent a great deal of time trying to protect them. (Courtesy Arcadia Historical Society.)

JENNY AIRCRAFT, c. 1919. The two-seater Curtis Jenny biplane, with a top-speed of only 75 miles per hour, was widely used to train pilots in the United States and Canada in World War I. Since most of the more than 6,000 planes manufactured were not equipped with weapons, they were sold to civilians following the war. (Courtesy Arcadia Historical Society.)

BALLOON SHEDS, C. 1918. This image offers an overview of the Ross Field facility. The white tents in the foreground were balloon sheds (tents) where maintenance was done on the balloons each night before they were "put to bed." The building near the center of the photograph was the YMCA. The one in the northern part of the field near the flagpole served as headquarters. The school's swimming pool, formerly a water reservoir, is just out of sight to the north. (Courtesy Arcadia Historical Society.)

BALLOON DISASTER, C. 1918. With three inflatable tail fins, Caquot balloons were quite stable as long as they faced into the wind. Occasionally, however, gusty or high winds could cause them to spiral and fall. In the disaster pictured here, the reconnaissance pilot almost certainly parachuted to safety. In France, the cause of balloon failure was usually associated with a fire caused by an enemy tracer shot into the balloon's hydrogen gas. With only a few seconds to jump before being engulfed by the burning balloon, they had to react instantly to an attack. Even then, it was possible for burning pieces of the balloon to set the pilot's parachute on fire, causing him to fall 1,000 or more feet to his death. (Courtesy Arcadia Historical Society.)

Five

POULTRY BRINGS PROSPERITY

The two decades following World War I marked the start of a new era in Arcadia. The burgeoning city's population had more than tripled, and it was struggling to cope with end-of-war inflation and growing pains caused by the rapid shift from a rural, farming economy to one based on manufacturing and services.

With the influx of new residents—many of whom arrived from large cities—came a demand for smaller homesites and services such as schools, postal delivery, utilities, and paved streets. Ironically, the one major improvement Arcadians refused to approve was the installation of a sewer system, a fact that prevented major industries from investing in the city until the 1940s.

Arcadia's government was preoccupied with fund-raising, while real estate developers focused on creating residential subdivisions and establishing a new business center on the west side of town. One such developer was R. H. "Rudy" Schwarzkopf, a poultry farmer turned real estate mogul, who arrived in 1910. Schwarzkopf understood the science of raising chickens and passed his enthusiasm on to many of his real estate clients. Chicken farming appealed to newcomers for several reasons: set-up costs were relatively low, the demand for eggs and meat was high, and the birds were perceived as a low maintenance crop. That many underestimated the hard work and risks involved did not deter Schwarzkopf. It wasn't long before he was the "go to" man for would-be chicken farmers, selling them everything from land to chicken coops.

To say that poultry was big business in Arcadia during the 1920s and 1930s would be an understatement. By the middle of the 1920s, the city had become known as the "egg basket" of Los Angeles, supplying some 5,000 eggs a day to big city markets. The infusion of funds provided by poultry farmers enabled growth in other areas of Arcadia as well, including schools, recreational facilities, and shopping centers, and set the stage for the economic boom Arcadia would experience in the 1930s as it recovered from the hardships and political wrangling brought on by the Great Depression.

THE CITY TAKES SHAPE. This photograph looks east on Huntington Drive at Santa Anita Avenue. Arcadia's first church, First Presbyterian Church of Arcadia, is on the left corner. City hall is farther down the road. By this point, electricity, streetlights, and sidewalks have been added. Note the street sign suspended by cables at the top of the picture. (Courtesy Arcadia Public Library.)

GASOLINE FUELS DEVELOPMENT, C. 1920. As more cars took to the road, businessmen like Bruce Wetmore invested in gas stations. Wetmore, who was active in the community, is shown standing in front of his station with his hands behind his back. Note the inflatable tire tubes leaning against the building and the glass cylinders at the top of the gas pumps advertising "filtered gas." (Courtesy Arcadia Public Library.)

POULTRY SPELLS PROSPERITY, C. 1920. Chickens scratch for food at one of the many poultry-raising facilities that sprang up in Arcadia during the 1920s and 1930s. Raising chickens was so popular that brochures advertising the city's attributes included the line, "Chickens do well in Arcadia—so do folks who raise 'em." (Courtesy Arcadia Public Library.)

GRADUATION DAY, C. 1920. The line of young girls pictured here is taking part in a graduation-day celebration in front of the soon-to-be-finished Arcadia Grammar School. The school was undergoing a face lift following the 1933 Long Beach earthquake, and the original Grecian pillars had been removed. (Courtesy Arcadia Public Library.)

A Tree Bordered Street

HIGHLIGHTS OF ARCADIA, 1920. This brochure was designed to sell prospective residents on Arcadia's virtues. The excellent climate, water, and soil (ideal for raising chickens), attractive homes, and "modern conveniences of living" were all touted. The "spirit of contentment and thrift" exhibited by the residents was also praised. Small wonder Arcadia's population grew by leaps and bounds in the 1920s and 1930s. (Courtesy Arcadia Public Library.)

BALDWIN AVENUE BEGINNINGS, C. 1923. This photograph looks north on Baldwin Avenue and illustrates how rural the Arcadia landscape was in the early 1920s. Anyone who has driven the modern, four-lane version of Baldwin Avenue can attest to the fact that the city's infrastructure has improved considerably. (Courtesy Arcadia Public Library.)

EARLY HOMES, C. 1922. When it came to building homes, the residents of Arcadia favored simple, rather old-fashioned designs that were spacious and comfortable. This photograph illustrates how rapidly Arcadia was growing and how much basic amenities, such as sidewalks and streetlights, were needed. (Courtesy Arcadia Public Library.)

THE SMILE OF SUCCESS. This is the friendly face of the owner of Ericsson's Pharmacy, Ralph B. Ericsson. He is leaning against the store's display case where Roi Tan Cigars are advertised. Located on the corner of Baldwin Avenue and Duarte Road, the shop began filling prescriptions for Arcadia residents in the early 1920s. (Courtesy Arcadia Historical Society.)

ANITA BALDWIN'S HERD, C. 1922. James Carpenter, the ranch manager for Anita Baldwin, is shown here with some of the mules and horses he cared for. Like her father before her, Anita Baldwin loved and bred a variety of horses, including Thoroughbreds, Arabians, and Percherons. (Courtesy Arcadia Historical Society.)

A WORKING TEAM, C. 1922. This team of mules and men was one of many that worked on Anita Baldwin's Anoakia Stock and Breeding Farm. Note how large the wagons were in relation to the men and the mules. (Courtesy Arcadia Historical Society.)

ARCADIA CITY HALL, C. 1927. Arcadia city officials, including members of the police, fire, engineering, and city clerk's departments, pose in front of city hall on the corner of Huntington Drive and First Avenue. Note the scenic, tree-lined view of the San Gabriel Mountains and the glass streetlamps on their cement columns. (Courtesy Arcadia Public Library.)

FIRST DAY OF SCHOOL, C. 1930. Arcadia Grammar School students are on their best behavior as they pose for the camera in front of their classroom on the first day of school. Like all kids, they look thoroughly uncomfortable in their new school clothes. (Courtesy Arcadia Historical Society.)

THE URBAN FAMILY, C. 1926. The Urbans were one of Arcadia's earliest families. Joseph and his wife, Barbara, were originally from Hungary. They arrived in the United States in 1903 and became citizens in 1909. They are shown here with their three children—from left to right, Emily, Tillie, and Roberta—on the steps of their home on Longden Avenue. (Courtesy Arcadia Historical Society.)

AN ARCADIA ICON, C. 1927. Helen Jackson, pictured sitting on the hood of her family's car with her mother's help, grew up to become a renowned master quilter whose work appeared throughout Southern California. Jackson also taught quilting classes for many years in Arcadia. (Courtesy Arcadia Historical Society.)

TRAGEDY STRIKES, c. 1927. This is the police car driven by the only Arcadia police officer ever killed in the line of duty. On July 18, 1927, officer Albert Mathies was patrolling with his partner when he noticed a car parked near the corner of Northview and Laurel Avenues. When he stopped to investigate, he was shot and killed by the car's occupants. (Courtesy Arcadia Public Library.)

EARLY POLICE FORCE, c. 1931. Pictured here are police chief Jack Richards (third from left) and four of his deputies. Richards was appointed police chief in November 1930. Prior to this, both the police and fire departments were overseen by the city marshal. Under Richards's stewardship, the police department moved from city hall into its own facility at 50 Wheeler Street. (Courtesy Arcadia Public Library.)

A MODEL SCHOOL. In the early 1920s, West Arcadia became a premier residential area with proximity to the "Red Car" line. Arcadia Grammar School eventually became overcrowded, and acreage on the southeast corner of Duarte Road and Holly Avenue was purchased from Clara Baldwin Stocker. A school opened in September 1927 with classrooms for grades one to six. In 1938, a kindergarten room was added, and in 1939, another addition resulted in 25 classrooms

HOLLY AVE. G.S.
ARCADIA, CALIF.
10-2-33

and an auditorium. Over time, Holly Avenue School's enrollment has increased to 722 students taught by 34 teachers, and a youth hut and tennis courts have been added. Former Holly Avenue principal Elsie Porri remembers how beautiful the grounds were, saying, "In the springtime, intermingled with extensive vegetable gardens . . . were California Poppies as far as the eye could see." (Courtesy Arcadia Historical Society.)

RURAL ARCADIA, C. 1931. Arcadia's rural roots are clearly visible in this photograph of a home built beside an orchard. Though the home is large and spacious, no attempts have been made to landscape the grounds or pave the roadway to the right of the house. It would be some years before the sophisticated, polished neighborhoods Arcadia is known for would emerge. (Courtesy Arcadia Historical Society.)

ARCADIA'S FIRST MALL, C. 1934. Arcadia's first mall was located on the southwest corner of Huntington Drive and First Avenue. Known as the Arcadia Drive-In Market, its shops were placed in an L shape around a gas station on the corner. This arrangement allowed customers to drive in, park, and visit any or all of the stores without moving their cars. (Courtesy Arcadia Public Library.)

66

A New Museum.
Visitors to William
Parker Lyon's
Pony Express
Museum received
this pamphlet.
A consummate
collector, Lyon
was fascinated by
the Old West. The
25¢ he charged
visitors to view his
collections seemed
like a bargain
when word got
out that one-of-
a-kind artifacts,
such as Ulysses S.
Grant's whiskey
glass and hundreds
of his cigar butts,
were on display.
(Courtesy Arcadia
Public Library.)

Lyon Pony Express WELLS FARGO Museum
130 W. Huntington Dr. (Santa Anita), Arcadia
U. S. HIGHWAY 66

A MILLION - DOLLAR WILD WEST
COLLECTION made by W. Parker Lyon
over a period of Forty Years.

24 Rooms of Genuine Gold-Rush Days Relics
from Fifty Abandoned Mining Towns
of California

OPEN DAILY FROM 8:00 A. M. to 6:00 P. M.
ADULTS 25c—CHILDREN 10c—Babies FREE

EASY TO REACH . . . FOLLOW THE MAP
U. S. HIGHWAY 66

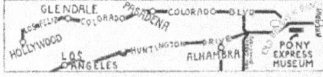

—or Pacific Electric (Monrovia Line from Los Angeles
Main Street Station) direct to Pony Express Station, on
the Old "Lucky" Baldwin Rancho. Directly opposite the
Museum is the great, modern Santa Anita Playground.

SOME MUSEUM EXHIBITS TO BE SEEN

Five Old Concord Stages; Five Ancient Hand-drawn
Fire Engines; Old Spanish Cannon; Huge Locks;
Hundreds of Famous Revolvers and Rifles; Fifty Sets
of Gold Scales; Complete Printing Office with Wash-
ington Hand Press; Indian Room with over 20,000
Specimens; Old Wells-Fargo Express Office; Fifty
Bullet-scarred Treasure Boxes; Photographs of Bandit
Hangings; Indian Scalps, Skulls, etc.; Gold Mining
Machinery and Gold Specimens; Complete Chinese
Joss House; Old Stores from Mining Towns, filled with
Pioneer Objects of Wearing Apparel; Complete Bar-
room moved at expense of over $10,000; Roulette, Lot-
tery, and Faro Layouts used in Early Mining Camps;
Early American Glass; Overlay Bohemian Lamps;
and thousands of other curiosities, many of which can
be found nowhere else in the country.

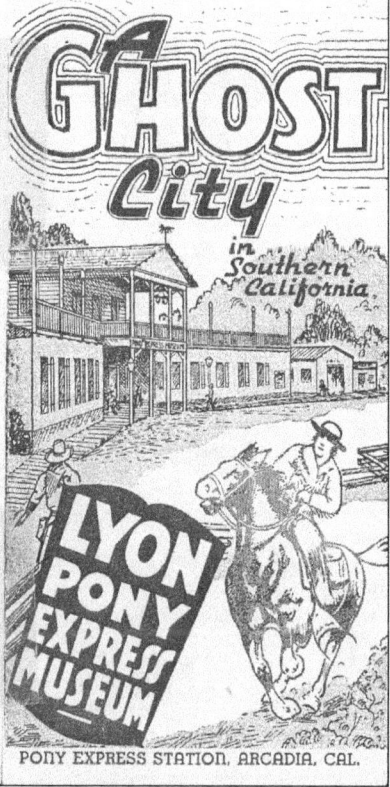

GHOST City in Southern California

LYON PONY EXPRESS MUSEUM

PONY EXPRESS STATION, ARCADIA, CAL.

Horse Racing Commemorated. The building that would become the Derby was purchased in 1938 by George Woolf, the jockey who rode to fame on Seabiscuit. Woolf envisioned a restaurant where jockeys and fans could gather and enjoy a good meal. The Derby features cowboy and horse racing memorabilia, including Seabiscuit's saddle, horseshoes, and photographs of his life and races. (Courtesy Arcadia Public Library.)

VIEW OF RACETRACK, C. 1930. In this aerial photograph of the Arcadia area, the massive scope of the Santa Anita Park's racetrack, stables, parking lots, and training area are clear. The track first opened its turnstiles on December 25, 1934. Today the training track seen in the bottom left section of the picture has been replaced by the Westfield Santa Anita shopping mall. (Courtesy Arcadia Public Library.)

RACETRACK SUCCESS, C. 1935. By 1934, Lucky Baldwin's dream of a profitable, top-flight racetrack had become a reality, as this packed parking lot clearly illustrates. The popularity of Thoroughbred racing soared in Southern California. Santa Anita Park regularly drew crowds of 50,000 to 60,000 race fans a day. (Courtesy Archives of the Pasadena Museum of History.)

WETMORE GETS A FACE LIFT. By 1935, Bruce Wetmore's gas station had become a bona fide service station with upgraded pumps, service bays, and a red-tile roof. Note that the lot has also been paved and landscaped, making it much more attractive to Wetmore's customers. (Courtesy Arcadia Public Library.)

FARM MEETS CITY, C. 1939. In sharp contrast to Arcadia's vision of itself as a modern, sophisticated city was the farmland that continued to exist within its boundaries. Pictured here is the produce stand on the corner of Las Tunas Drive and Santa Anita Avenue where owner Carl Kophamer and his family sold the corn they raised. (Courtesy Arcadia Public Library.)

DAIRY DAYS, C. 1938. The cattle pictured here are grazing on what used to be Supreme Dairy property. The dairy took over in 1923 when Anita Baldwin abandoned her stock-breeding operations and her large barn became available. Cattle, chicken, and hog farms were eventually forced out of business after citizens complained about the smell. Hugo Reid Elementary School currently occupies the site. (Courtesy Arcadia Public Library.)

ATTENDING THE SHERIFF'S BARBECUE. Pictured here is young Jerry Selmer attending Sheriff Eugene Biscailuz's annual barbecue held at Santa Anita Park. Sheriff Biscailuz was sheriff of Los Angeles County from 1934 to 1958 and was an admired and popular figure within the Arcadia community. (Courtesy Selmer family collection.)

SANTA ANITA PARK HEYDAY. This is a 1939 photograph of the grandstands at Santa Anita Park. Known for its elegance, the park has been the setting for many historical races and numerous movies, including *Seabiscuit*. Note the lovely art deco details in the building's facade. (Courtesy Arcadia Public Library.)

TOPPERS, C. 1941. As automobiles became an integral part of life in Arcadia, businesses responded by making services easier to access by car. Pictured here is Toppers, one of the first restaurants to cater to the drive-in craze. It was located on the northwest corner of Baldwin Avenue and Huntington Drive and was particularly popular with Arcadia's youth. (Courtesy Arcadia Historical Society.)

NEW ARCADIA THEATRE

GRAND OPENING DECEMBER 23

Coming Attractions

"COUNT OF MONTE CRISTO"   "GAY DIVORCEE"
"WHITE PARADE"   "ST. LOUIS KID"
"KENTUCK KERNELS"

ARCADIA THEATRE PROGRAM, C. 1924. This leaflet announced programs at the new Arcadia Theatre on Huntington Drive. The theater's owner planned to compete with businesses on the west side of town. Due to safety concerns, however, construction was temporarily halted. Though it was eventually completed, the theater remained controversial. When it burned down in 1944, the permit to restore it was denied. (Courtesy Arcadia Public Library.)

PLANNING FOR WATER, C. 1927. Built by the Los Angeles County Public Works Department Flood Control District, the Santa Anita Dam was part of the county's efforts to store municipal water and to hold back debris. The dam was completed in 1927. (Courtesy Arcadia Public Library.)

Six

ARCADIA BECOMES
A DESTINATION

Even before Arcadia became a city in 1903, the area was attracting visitors from across the country and nations as far removed as Denmark. They came to do business, enjoy the scenery, and bask in the glow of Lucky Baldwin's larger-than-life personality. The area's physical attributes—fertile soil, artesian wells, and scenic views—were also widely publicized in newspapers, increasing the town's appeal to investors and tourists alike.

By the 1930s, things had changed dramatically for Arcadia. Not only had its founder passed away, setting the stage for a complete turnaround in government, but the weight of the Great Depression had descended on the community. Jobs were scarce, money tight, and the city still lacked some basic amenities that would allow it to compete for tourist and industrial dollars.

Fortunately, Arcadians have never lacked vision, and several ambitious projects combined to help pull the city out of its slump. The first was the completion of Santa Anita Park. This classy, professionally run track was a success from the day it opened on Christmas Day in 1934. The second was the opening of William Parker Lyon's Pony Express Museum, which drew hundreds of thousands of visitors with its collections of Western memorabilia.

Finally, thanks to the efforts of Rep. John Hoeppel (an Arcadia resident) the War Department sold Ross Field back to Los Angeles County. The county, in turn, applied to the Works Progress Administration (WPA) for the funds needed to turn the 185 acres into a recreational facility. The resulting two-year project generated jobs, poured much-needed funds into the city, and produced top-flight tennis courts, lawn bowling greens, a baseball diamond, an Olympic-size swimming pool, and an 18-hole golf course.

Today, in addition to the racetrack and recreational park, Arcadia is home to the award-winning Los Angeles County Arboretum and Botanic Gardens, where the Queen Anne Cottage and Coach Barn are preserved.

PONY EXPRESS MUSEUM, C. 1938. William Parker Lyon, the founder of Lyon Van and Storage Company, was the creator of the first Pony Express Museum. Lyon moved the museum from San Marino to Arcadia in 1934 after his collection outgrew its space. The museum's new home was on six acres purchased from Anita Baldwin. Included in the museum's collection were items acquired from an old safe Lyon purchased and blew open: over $2,000 in gold coins, unused Pony Express stamps, and gold dust. These contents began Lyon's interest in Western memorabilia. He visited ghost towns, mining camps, and small towns, collecting artifacts such as old signs, bottles, clothing, saddlebags, pictures, chamber pots, stagecoaches, dishes, and even a jail cell. His museum was an instant success and drew record crowds until its closure in 1955. (Courtesy Arcadia Public Library.)

MUSEUM INTERIOR, C. 1938. This photograph shows two rooms in William Parker Lyon's Pony Express Museum, located across from Santa Anita Park on the corner of Huntington Drive and Colorado Boulevard. Admission was set at 25¢ for adults. To accommodate his more than one million collectibles, Lyon constructed three enormous buildings, the largest with 30 rooms, some with themes. One room might contain saloon items, another whale oil and kerosene lamps. Other themes were based on shotguns, dolls, toys, clothing, iron boxes, musical instruments, "wanted" posters, stagecoaches, and even a Chinese joss house. Among collectors, Lyon's collection of Native American artifacts was considered one of the nation's finest. (Courtesy Arcadia Public Library.)

LYON'S GENERAL STORE, C. 1937. The general store in William Parker Lyon's Pony Express Museum contained items from abandoned stores in the California Gold Rush region and Nevada. Several rooms contained shoes, bags, hats, and other apparel. Other rooms contained stoves, a large lamp collection, chamber pots, dishes, pots, guns, a pharmacy, and a wooden American Indian. A consummate extrovert, Lyon frequently posed for photographs in his rooms. In this particular photograph, he is seen trying on a lady's hat. One source estimates that the general store alone had over one million artifacts. (Courtesy Arcadia Public Library.)

LYON'S PONY EXPRESS SALOON. A popular attraction in the Pony Express Museum was an authentic Western saloon with gaming tables, swinging doors, old signs, brass spittoons (gaboons), card tables, a long bar, and a roulette wheel. The hanging rope, pistols, cards, "wanted" posters, and whiskey bottles fit with the California Gold Rush theme. The room's elaborate chandelier added a sense of grandeur and authenticity. The museum also had a pawnshop and pharmacy for those whose luck had run out. The bar dated back to when gold was discovered at Sutter's Mill in California. Lyon bought everything that struck his fancy for almost 50 years. His collections were enormous and eclectic. (Courtesy Arcadia Public Library.)

VINTAGE TRAIN. In 1939, in an effort to attract visitors to his museum, William Parker Lyon purchased an abandoned narrow-gauge train from Nevada and constructed a circular track on his property. It wasn't long before he began offering short rides to museum visitors. He called the ride the "Haw Haw Route." Later he purchased Arcadia's Southern Pacific depot and added it to his museum as well. (Courtesy Arcadia Public Library.)

PRINTING PRESS, c. 1939. Here Lyon poses with an old printing press. The room holding the press was filled with printing supplies from the mid-1800s. After Lyon's death, the museum was sold to Bill Harrah and moved to Reno, Nevada. Because of its size, many of the artifacts were never displayed. The collection was eventually broken up and sold to private investors. (Courtesy Arcadia Public Library.)

TALLAC KNOLL, ARCADIA ARBORETUM. In 1936, Anita Baldwin sold 1,300 acres of the old Baldwin Ranch to Harry Chandler, owner of the *Los Angeles Times*. In 1943, Tallac Knoll, one of the most spacious and beautifully landscaped locations on the former rancho, was being subdivided and readied for sale by Rancho Santa Anita, Inc. Street maps had already been drawn up and lots were about to be put on the market when the County of Los Angeles, Arboretum Committee, and State of California stepped in to preserve a portion of the estate. Together they purchased 111 acres for $320,000. Included in the purchase was the old Baldwin homesite with the Hugo Reid Adobe, Queen Anne Cottage, Baldwin Lake, and ranch buildings. This complex became the Los Angeles State and County Arboretum in 1947. (Courtesy Arcadia Historical Society.)

FILMING *DEVIL'S ISLAND*, C. 1940. Hollywood took full advantage of the unique settings the arboretum had to offer. Several motion pictures were filmed there, including *The Road to Singapore* (1940), *Notorious* (1946) with Ingrid Bergman, and *The African Queen* (1951) starring Humphrey Bogart and Katherine Hepburn. This photograph shows the filming of *Devil's Island* (1940) starring Boris Karloff. Film and television companies continue to use the arboretum today. (Courtesy Arcadia Public Library.)

TONGVA REED HUT, C. 1975. Arcadia's earliest inhabitants were the Tongva Indians. The Spaniards called this tribe the Gabrielinos during the mission period. The sites of their homes were known as Aleupkigna. These Native Americans lived in structures made of willow poles and thatched layers of reed. Replicas of these structures, known as kiiys or wickiups, were built near the Hugo Reid Adobe in the early 1960s. (Courtesy Arcadia Pubic Library.)

RESTORATION OF SANTA FE DEPOT. Concerned citizens and the Arcadia Historical Society were instrumental in moving the historic Santa Fe Depot to the arboretum in the late 1960s. The depot was in the path of the I-210 or Foothill Freeway and was about to be demolished. Unlike many Santa Fe stations, this two-story depot was constructed of bricks—manufactured at Baldwin's brick factory. The depot was dismantled brick by brick and replicated using some of the original building materials on the arboretum grounds just west of Baldwin Avenue and east of the Hugo Reid Adobe. The depot was originally built for Lucky Baldwin, who agreed on tracks through his property if trains would stop at his ranch. He used the depot as his personal welcoming station. The bottom floor of the depot contained the agent's office and baggage room. A bedroom and parlor were upstairs. Today the depot is furnished, but the only original piece of furniture is an 1890s desk owned by a former stationmaster. (Courtesy Arcadia Public Library.)

BALDWIN LAKE, 2007. Here Baldwin Lake (the lagoon) appears with the Queen Anne Cottage behind it. This spot is a favorite with photographers. The lake has been used as the backdrop for several films, including *Meet the Fockers* in 2004. Sixty percent of the ranch received water from artesian sources, including the old lily pond on the south side of the Queen Anne Cottage. (Courtesy Arcadia Historical Society.)

TROPICAL JUNGLE, 2007. An entrance to the arboretum's tropical jungle is shown here. When Harry Chandler took over the property he purchased from Anita Baldwin in 1936, he began allowing motion-picture companies to rent the property for filming. Four of the Johnny Weissmuller *Tarzan* movies were filmed in the arboretum's lagoon and jungle settings in the late 1950s. (Courtesy Arcadia Historical Society.)

AERIAL VIEW OF RACETRACKS. This aerial photograph of Santa Anita Park shows two tracks. The first track (top right) was begun in 1932 by Anita Baldwin and her business partner, Joe Smoot. The project was abandoned in 1933 when Smoot left Arcadia. The second track was begun in 1934 after Anita sold 214 acres to the Los Angeles Turf Club (LATC). The new track was located just east of the first. In 1938, a training track was added to the facility just to the right of the horse barns seen above. This training track (not shown) was known as "La Chiquita" and was eliminated when the Santa Anita Fashion Park mall was constructed in the mid-1970s. (Courtesy Arcadia Public Library.)

SANTA ANITA PARK
GRANDSTAND. Opening
day at Santa Anita Park
was on December 25,
1934. A near-capacity
crowd was on hand to
watch the eight races
on the card. The track's
architect, Gordon
Kaufman, received an
international award for
his work. Meticulous
landscaping, top-flight
stables, and stunning
views of the San
Gabriel Mountains
have contributed to the
track's ongoing success.
(Courtesy Arcadia
Historical Society.)

THE SPORT OF KINGS. In 1935, Santa Anita Park held its first $100,000 stakes race: the Santa
Anita Handicap. One of the richest purses in the United States, it is still a major highlight of the
park's racing season. Santa Anita Park also pioneered the use of photo-finish cameras and was
the first to offer racing on turf in the United States. (Courtesy Arcadia Public Library.)

JAPANESE RELOCATION CENTER, 1942. In February 1942, President Roosevelt signed Executive Order No. 9066 authorizing the War Department to "exclude any persons who constituted a danger to the United States from military areas." Since the United States was at war with Japan, all persons of Japanese ancestry were considered dangerous. To accommodate the thousands of people the government believed were threats, Santa Anita Park was turned into a relocation facility. By April 1942, some 400 buildings had been erected and internees began to arrive. Within two months, over 12,000 Japanese were in the camp. By September, however, they had been relocated to facilities farther inland. The park was then turned into an army ordnance training center. Twenty thousand soldiers moved in and began training. (Courtesy Arcadia Public Library.)

GEORGE WOOLF STATUE, C. 1950. George Woolf was one of the nation's leading jockeys between 1928 and 1946. His ability to perform under pressure earned him the nickname "The Iceman." His most famous race was the history-making match-race between Seabiscuit and War Admiral, which he and Seabiscuit won decisively. Woolf's career ended in 1946 after a fall from which he never recovered. (Courtesy Arcadia Historical Society.)

LOS ANGELES COUNTY'S ARCADIA PARK. When Ross Field was closed, the War Department sold the property to Los Angeles County with the stipulation that it be used for recreational purposes. The result is the 185-acre park containing tennis courts, ball fields, lawn bowling greens, a pool, and a golf course. Most of the work was done by the Works Progress Administration (WPA). (Courtesy Arcadia Historical Society.)

LAWN BOWLING, C. 1940. The Santa Anita Bowling Green Club was organized in June 1937. Initially an all-male organization, it was eventually integrated 15 years later, though not without pressure from the women. The County of Los Angeles has made several improvements to the facility over the years, including two additional greens and a clubhouse. Today the park's four greens are considered some of the finest in the nation. (Courtesy Arcadia Historical Society.)

MEMORIAL FOUNTAIN, C. 2004. This fountain was designed in 1962 as a contribution to civic beautification and a memorial to those who gave their lives in war. It was refurbished in 2002 with new glass and mosaic tiles meant to resemble the patterns in peacock feathers. The fountain was topped with a large bronze peacock and rededicated to those who lost their lives on September 11, 2001. (Courtesy Arcadia Historical Society.)

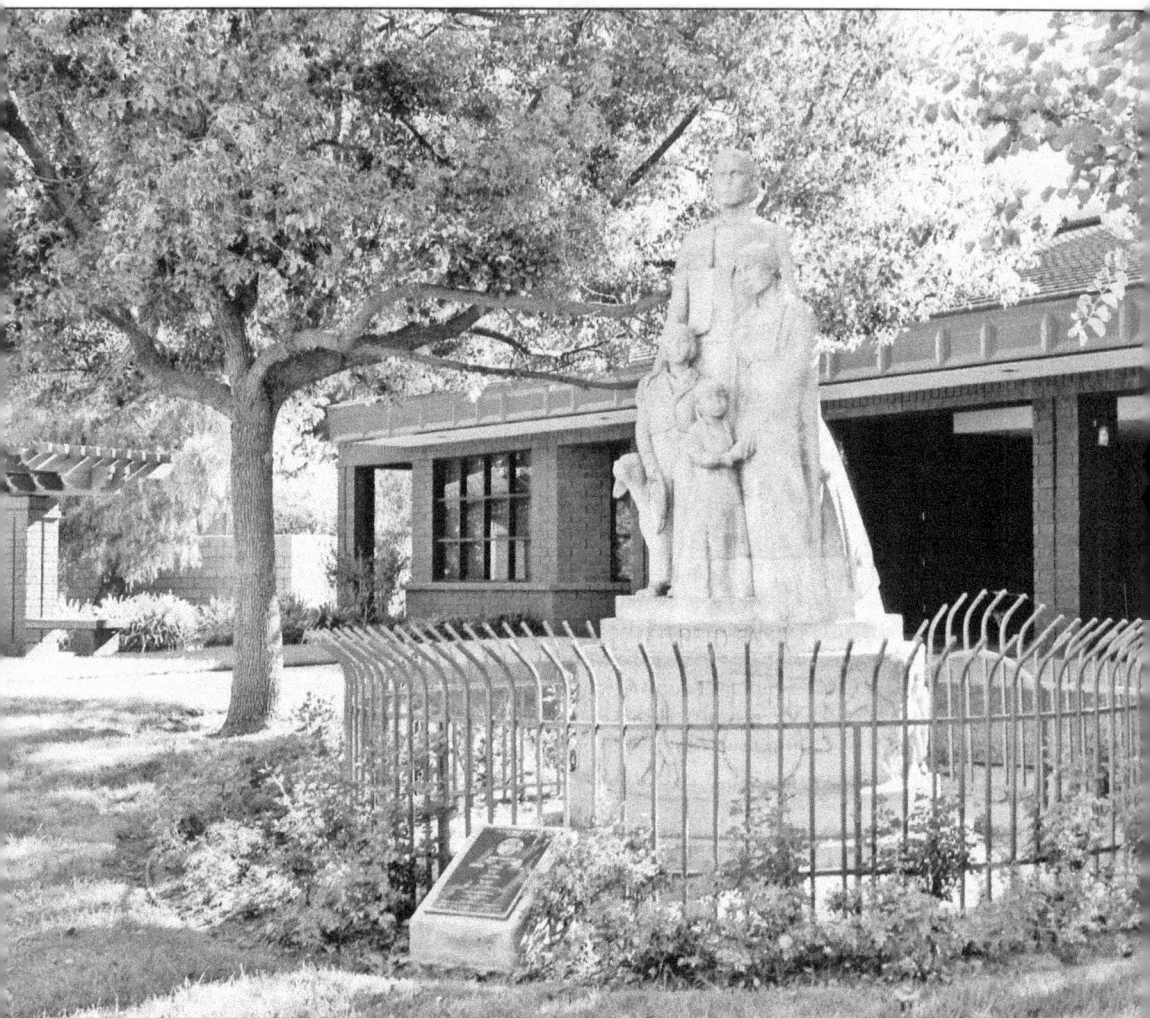

HUGO REID STATUE, C. 2006. This 1937 statue of Hugo Reid, his wife, Doña Victoria, and her two children, Maria Ygnacia and Carlitos, was originally placed in Los Angeles County's Arcadia Park. Reid was the first private owner of Santa Anita Rancho and is credited with building the first permanent home in Arcadia. Reid also wrote a series of 22 essays on the culture of Native Americans in Los Angeles County. These essays have become original source material for anthropologists. Reid's adobe is reconstructed in the arboretum near Baldwin's Queen Anne Cottage and Baldwin Lake. The statue of Reid and his family was executed by Preston L. Prescott. In 2001, after over 60 years in Arcadia Park, the Arcadia Historical Society proposed that the statue be moved and restored. In 2003, the 30,000-pound statue was successfully restored and relocated to a site adjacent to the Ruth and Charles Gilb Arcadia Historical Museum. (Courtesy Arcadia Historical Society.)

Seven

A City in Transition

As World War II came to an end, and Arcadia's population continued to grow by leaps and bounds (up by 70 percent in just six years), the city was confronted with some real and pressing problems. Chief among the concerns were the long-overdue sewer and flood-control systems. For years, Arcadia residents had balked at the expense of installing sewer lines and drainage ditches. However, the influx of new residents made both a priority. After heated debates, the issue of how to pay for these improvements was resolved in 1948. A bond election was held, and Arcadia could finally afford modern sanitation.

Another major concern was the strain new residents were putting on the public schools. Classrooms were full to bursting, and it was clear that something had to be done immediately. Fortunately, Arcadia's civic leaders were both practical and proactive. Beginning in 1947, new schools were built almost yearly until 1960. In addition, foreseeing an increased demand for housing, large vacant sections of land that had once been devoted to orchards, truck gardens, and chickens were subdivided, cleared, and laid out as streets. Homes of all sizes followed in the 1950s, going up as fast as building supplies became available.

Along with new homes came neighborhoods and homeowner associations. The Gardens, a subdivision built with curving streets around a central plan, was a good example of how these concepts were implemented. For the first time, certain parts of Arcadia became more fashionable than others. The Highlands, a development just north of Foothill Boulevard, lead the way as the "premier" residential area. Likewise, the land sold by Anita Baldwin to the Chandler interests in 1936 was considered very desirable.

Finally, conscious of the city's outward persona, Arcadia's leaders turned their attention to public buildings and attractions. A new city hall was constructed in 1948, Lucky Baldwin's former home became the arboretum in 1952, and a new public library was built in 1961. In the end, Arcadia's transformation into one of the most prestigious communities in Southern California took less than 20 years—not bad for a town whose prior claim to fame was chickens.

LOOKING NORTH ON FIRST AVENUE. The original city hall building shown here served Arcadia well for 28 years. By 1946, however, additional space was needed. Five locations were considered before the current site between the racetrack and Los Angeles County's Arcadia Park was selected. Hiram Unruh's home was located behind the "Floral Designs" sign and was demolished in the late 1940s. (Courtesy Arcadia Historical Society.)

ARCADIA CITY HALL, 1960S. After years of debate about where to construct the new city hall building, land owned by Rancho Santa Anita Corporation was purchased. Few complained about the cost ($39,324), but many were unhappy about the location. Neither new taxes nor bonded indebtedness were required to finance it. The building cost $211,387 to construct. (Courtesy Arcadia Historical Society.)

PEACH BLOSSOM PARADE. The Peach Blossom Festival was organized in 1949 to coincide with the dedication of city hall and the civic center. Local florist Hortense Seymore organized the festival. The daylong celebration included a parade, picnic, and dance, and a grove of flowering peach trees was planted behind city hall in honor of the veterans of World War II. (Courtesy Arcadia Public Library.)

PROUD OF ARCADIA, C. 1950. This display, created by the Arcadia Chamber of Commerce, called attention to the many outstanding amenities Arcadia residents enjoyed. The theme, "Designed with You in Mind," highlights some of the latest civic improvements, including the newly installed sewer system and city hall. (Courtesy Arcadia Historical Society.)

GOING TO THE RACES, 1952. Following World War II, gasoline rationing ended and Santa Anita Park once again became popular with racing fans and the Hollywood elite. Cars would line up along Huntington Drive and Baldwin Avenue to get into the park. Notice that the Pacific Electric Railway tracks have been removed but not yet replaced by landscaping. (Courtesy Arcadia Public Library.)

HARNESS RACING, 1963. This was the most popular form of racing in the 1800s. Drivers, riding in fragile two-wheeled carts called "sulkies," controlled their horses by voice and reins. The horses were either trotters or pacers. Trotters have diagonal gaits, and pacers (also called "Side-wheelers") have parallel gaits. A great deal of time and patience is required to train trotters and pacers to race. (Courtesy Arcadia Public Library.)

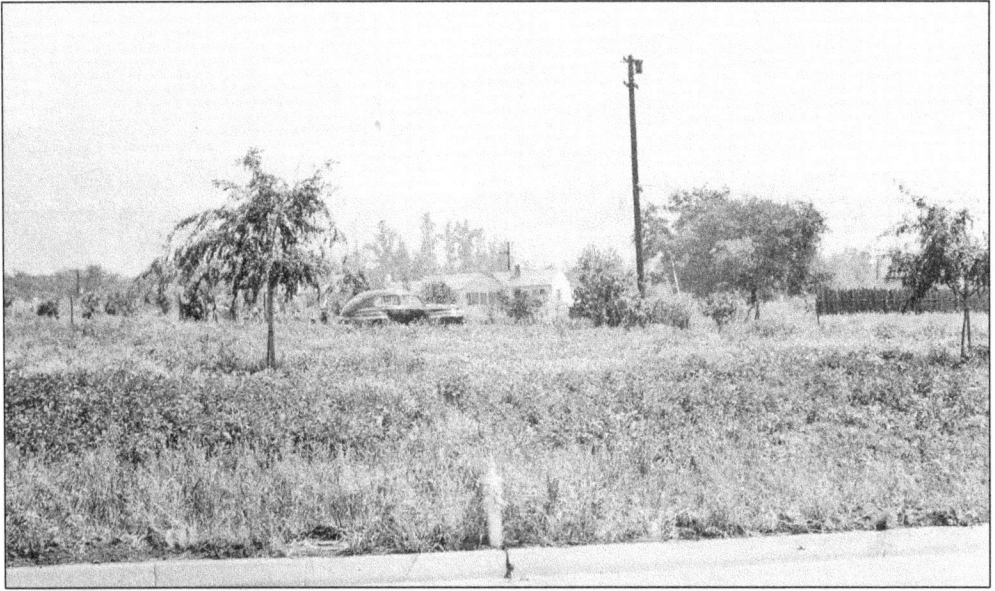

AN AREA IN TRANSITION. This photograph was taken in 1946 from Huntington Drive looking north over the acres of undeveloped land that would become Santa Anita Village. Another major housing boom had just begun, with large parcels of land being subdivided and streets paved. Note that this area was already supplied with water and electricity. Several new homes can be seen beyond the car. (Courtesy Arcadia Historical Society.)

A VILLAGE HOME IN 1960. The classic contemporary design pictured here was typical of the average Village home. Pride of ownership is apparent in the well-tended yard. A fad of the time was to have a gas lamppost installed in the front yard. (Courtesy Arcadia Historical Society.)

FLOOD CONTROL CHANNEL. Heavy winter rains used to flood large areas of Arcadia. After the legendary 1938 deluge, in which 15 inches fell in five days, city and county officials were determined to find a solution. Though nothing could be done before World War II, this channel was constructed soon thereafter. Running south through the racetrack and into El Monte, it directs water into catch basins. (Courtesy Arcadia Historical Society.)

ROAD PAVING, C. 1955. Not all streets in Arcadia had curbs and gutters, and most had no sidewalks. As this photographs shows, completing these projects was a monumental, ongoing task. Eastern sections of the city received attention in 1954 and 1956, and sidewalk construction was underway by the 1960s. (Courtesy Arcadia Historical Society.)

THE HIGHLANDS ROAD GRADING. Work began in earnest in the early 1950s on the Highlands development, which became a prime residential area with a strong homeowners' association. In this photograph, work is being done on the road that would become Highland Oaks Drive in the Elkins subdivision. Highland Oaks Drive winds its way north from Foothill Boulevard. (Courtesy Arcadia Historical Society.)

SOUTH ARCADIA BUSINESS. This 1963 photograph shows a rare expanse of open land between Las Tunas Drive and Live Oak Avenue. Tire shops, an upholstery store, an automotive parts and repair service, real estate offices, and a building supply store made up the eclectic mix of businesses on Live Oak Avenue. Carl Kophamer's corn stand was across the street on Las Tunas Drive. (Courtesy Arcadia Historical Society.)

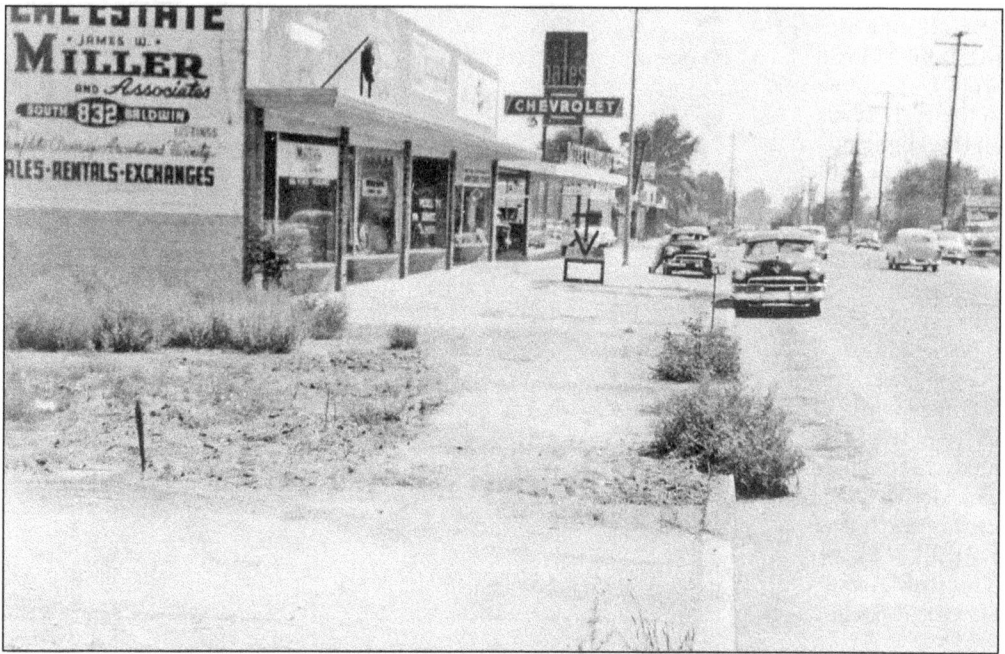

BALDWIN AVENUE, WEST ARCADIA, 1950S. Baldwin Avenue south of Huntington Drive looks neglected without sidewalks and with weeds growing unchecked. Clearly Arcadia still has a long way to go before becoming the clean, elegant city it is known as today. (Courtesy Arcadia Historical Society.)

FIRST AVENUE AND DUARTE ROAD. In the 1950s, as travel by automobile became increasingly popular, there appeared to be a gas station on almost every corner in every city in the nation. Arcadia was no exception. Today traffic signals have replaced the stop signs and sidewalks are being laid out. (Courtesy Arcadia Historical Society.)

SHOPPING BAG'S GRAND OPENING. In the middle of the 1950s, when Hinshaw's Department Store was opened, West Arcadia became the shopping center of choice. This Shopping Bag was a modern supermarket sporting a large inventory, swift checkout, and a friendly staff. (Courtesy Arcadia Historical Society.)

APACHE PRINCESSES AND MARCHING BAND. This 1974 photograph shows the Arcadia High School marching band strutting its stuff in the Arcadia Invitational Parade, held on the last Saturday in November. West Arcadia "Hub" merchants and business owners organized the parade and accompanying events for many years. (Courtesy Parrille family.)

HORSES ON THE AVENUE, 1960S. Many Arcadia residents used to enjoy riding their horses along tree-lined Santa Anita Avenue (Double Drive). Equestrians could ride up into the mouth of the Santa Anita Canyon and stop to admire the spectacular view of the city and San Gabriel Valley below. (Courtesy Arcadia Historical Society.)

TURNQUIST DOG OBEDIENCE CLASSES, 1970S. Saturday mornings at Los Angeles County's Arcadia Park were devoted to dog training. Owners would bring their less than obedient dogs to the classes taught by members of the Turnquist family. Dogs of all breeds and all levels of ability could be seen. Not all dogs were accepted for training, and aggressive dogs were excused. (Courtesy Arcadia Historical Society.)

EL RANCHO SHOPPING CENTER. The first request for a shopping center on Huntington Drive between Michillinda Avenue and Sunset Boulevard was made in the late 1930s, but voters rejected it. Final approval wasn't given until 1948. The word "Michillinda" is a combination of *Michigan*, *Illinois*, and *Indiana*. It was created by developers from those three states who couldn't agree on a name for the area. (Courtesy Arcadia Public Library.)

METHODIST HOSPITAL, C. 1957. Methodist Hospital of Southern California is located on a 22-acre site leased from the City of Arcadia. It is a fully accredited hospital and a nonprofit charitable institution serving Arcadia's residents. The hospital has been continuously expanding since it opened in 1957. (Courtesy Arcadia Historical Society.)

FIRST PRESBYTERIAN CHURCH, 1956. Arcadia's first religious group was organized in 1914 with 24 members. For several years, the congregation had no regular place to meet. Then Anita Baldwin sold them the lots that contained the original packing-shed school. Members were finally able to construct a church in 1918. Additions were made to this building in 1934, and the church was later moved to First Avenue and Alice Street. (Courtesy Paul Geerlings.)

ARCADIA, C. 1963. An aerial photograph of the "Y" formed by Huntington Drive and Colorado Place shows the Flamingo Hotel in the lower right corner. The theater and Henry's Restaurant are located across the street. Lyon's Pony Express Museum previously occupied the land where the Flamingo Hotel is located. At the top of the picture, a portion of the hotel's garden area can be seen. (Courtesy Arcadia Historical Society.)

Eight

DENSITY AND DIVERSITY

To spend an afternoon navigating Arcadia's bustling streets or shopping in its thriving business sectors is to experience density and diversity directly. Home to more than 53,000 people, Arcadia is both heavily populated and racially mixed. In a single block on Baldwin Avenue, for example, it is possible to buy produce from a Japanese grocer, fill prescriptions at a Chinese pharmacy, order lunch in Spanish, Vietnamese, or Korean, and speak Croatian at Starbucks. The fact that most of these transplants speak their own innovative versions of English only adds to the multilingual stew.

Interestingly, racial diversity was built into Arcadia from the start. Lucky Baldwin employed an eclectic mix of nationalities: Mexicans to harvest his crops, blacks to tend his horses, Chinese to cook, and Basques to tend his sheep. Since then, immigrants have arrived in waves—Japanese in the 1920s and 1930s, Caucasians after World War II, and Chinese in the 1980s.

By contrast, density came rather late to Arcadia. The city's large tracts of land were divided gradually in response to economic demand. Originally an agricultural community, with 300- to 500-acre lots, Arcadia's first subdivisions occurred between 1912 and 1916 as new residents planted orchards and began raising chickens on 2- to 5-acre plots. As the demand for housing increased, Santa Anita Village and Baldwin Stocker Acres were developed in the late 1930s and early 1940s. Following World War II, smaller lots, built on land once planted in potatoes, caught on in the southeast portion of town. Meanwhile, above Foothill Boulevard, pricier projects such as the Highlands and Santa Anita Oaks took shape.

Today virtually every piece of land in Arcadia is occupied. The only way to construct new buildings is to tear older ones down. The question of what to preserve and what to sacrifice is constantly and hotly debated. This doesn't mean, however, that Arcadians have forsaken beauty. With 400 acres of undeveloped land at their city's core, and miniparks tucked into corners, Arcadia's residents enjoy the best of both worlds—economic prosperity and rural, old-world charm.

AN OLDER HOME, C. 1930S. This older home, located on Baldwin Avenue, is like a voice from the past. In sharp contrast to the large, multistory homes being built today, its simple box style, arched doorways and windows, and tile roof are reminiscent of the early missions. The property itself hasn't changed since the 1930s. (Courtesy Arcadia Historical Society.)

CLEARING SPACE FOR NEW GROWTH. With the help of a bulldozer, this lot is being cleared and prepared for a new home. Land in Arcadia has become so valuable that modest homes built prior to World War II are being demolished and replaced by palatial homes and condominiums, often several to a lot. This increased density has helped fuel Arcadia's population explosion. (Courtesy Arcadia Historical Society.)

HOUSING DENSITY. This image illustrates just how dense housing can become in Arcadia. Lots that once held single homes are now accommodating large-scale condominium complexes that house many families. One saddening consequence of this kind of development is that many if not most of the mature trees are removed when the complexes are built. (Courtesy Arcadia Historical Society.)

NEW HOME. This 10,000-square-foot home (built on three-fourths of an acre) represents the newest architectural trend in Arcadia's housing market. Many of these homes have been built by speculators and are beautifully landscaped. In keeping with the city's tree ordinance, mature oak trees are now protected from removal. This particular home is valued at more than $3 million in 2007. (Courtesy Arcadia Historical Society.)

DIVERSE SIGNAGE. Long-term residents of Arcadia are often bemused and entertained by the multilingual signs that appear as the city's population continues to diversify. Here two businesses on Duarte Road announce their presence in both Chinese and English. Elsewhere in town, it is possible to see signs in Japanese, Korean, and Vietnamese as well. (Courtesy Arcadia Historical Society.)

ETHNIC BUSINESSES. Like many businesses in Arcadia, the restaurants pictured here are advertising their wares in more than one language. One of the big benefits of diversification is the arrival of a variety of cultures and cuisines. Thanks to Arcadia's hungry, multinational population, the city is becoming known for its good food as well as its beauty. (Courtesy Arcadia Historical Society.)

LUCKY BALDWIN DAY, 2003. Whenever it is brought out for public events, Arcadia's restored vintage fire truck is a real crowd-pleaser, especially with the younger crowd. The smiling face of the child sitting in the driver's seat says it all. This city-sponsored event was held at Los Angeles County's Arcadia Park and attended by several thousand people. (Courtesy Teri Weeks.)

LUCKY BALDWIN PICNIC, 2003. This community event was popular with folks of all ages each year it was held. Balloons, games, and good food were staples. The mounted police, looking polished and official in their uniforms, also made an appearance. As this photograph illustrates, kids were thrilled to see the horses and adults took advantage of the opportunity to take great photographs. (Courtesy Teri Weeks.)

THE CENTENNIAL CELEBRATION. In 2003, Arcadia celebrated its first 100 years as a city. At one event, celebrating the city's diverse population, a fashion show was held. Featuring some of Arcadia's favorite residents dressed in authentic ethnic costumes from China, the event was a huge success as shown by the large smiles worn by Barbara and Gary Kovacic. (Courtesy the Kovacic family.)

CENTENNIAL CELEBRATION. In this photograph, some of the members of the Los Angeles Kimono Club are shown wearing their authentic Japanese attire. From left to right are Yaeko Hosobuchi, Tatsushi Nakamura, Carol Hyland, Fumi Akutagawa, Kyoko Nakamura, Yoshie Sato, Masako Kobashi, and Takeyuki Miyauchi. (Courtesy the Nakamura family.)

Nine

ARCADIA
THEN AND NOW

To say that Arcadia has changed since Lucky Baldwin managed to convince the citizens of his sleepy little township to vote for city-hood would be a huge understatement. A better word might be "transformed" or even "metamorphosed," as Arcadia has repeatedly reinvented itself—going from slow-paced rural obscurity to bustling urban notoriety.

Today Arcadia is home to some 53,000 souls living on some of the most sought-after real estate in California. Large sections of the city are devoted to lovely residential neighborhoods that have earned Arcadia the moniker "Community of Homes." Likewise, businesses of all kinds thrive in the commercial sections of town. But this was not always the case. As the photographs on these pages illustrate, there are dramatic differences between Arcadia in the 1890s (when photography first became available) and the Arcadia of today. With the exception of Santa Anita Park, the school on First Avenue, and Los Angeles County's Arcadia Park, the landscape of Arcadia has been malleable and shifting.

Responding to the demands and tastes of the city's diverse population, whole sections of Arcadia have received face lifts or been demolished and rebuilt. Restaurants, theaters, and stores have come and gone, leaving many longtime residents feeling shell-shocked and wondering, "What's next?"

The answer to that question lies, in part, in the photographs about to be seen. Look closely and notice the subtle shifts in perspective and priorities that have taken place over time. Look again, and a common thread can be found weaving its way through the decades—an excitement and sense of purpose that underlies everything the community undertakes.

This, then, is the defining heart of Arcadia—its gift, inherited from its visionary founder—the belief that "given hard work and determination, anything is possible."

DOUBLE DRIVE LOOKING NORTH. In the 1890s, Santa Anita Avenue (above) was a dirt path lined with four alternating rows of eucalyptus and pepper trees. It has grown into a heavily traveled, multilane thoroughfare, and the trees have been relegated to a single row in the central median (below). These photographs look north toward the San Gabriel Mountains from the intersection of Santa Anita Avenue and Huntington Drive (originally known as Falling Leaf Avenue). Eucalyptus and pepper trees were an integral part of E. J. "Lucky" Baldwin's vision for the city. Some 40,000 of these trees were planted along the streets of the residential developments Baldwin was promoting in the late 1880s. The tall white building (below) is the office tower at 15 North Santa Anita Avenue, the first high-rise building in Arcadia. (Above, courtesy Arcadia Public Library; below, Arcadia Historical Society.)

OAKWOOD HOTEL/24 HOUR FITNESS. The first and most prominent business to open on the land that would become Arcadia was Lucky Baldwin's Oakwood Hotel (pictured above in July 1890). Opened in 1887, the hotel stood on the southwest corner of First Avenue and East Santa Clara Street, across from the train depot. The two-story, brick building featured hot and cold running water and a fireplace in each of its 35 rooms. Other amenities included a fine restaurant, telegraph and phone connections, and a post office. The Oakwood was destroyed by fire in 1911, two years after Baldwin's death. Today the site is occupied by the two-story, 44,000-square-foot 24 Hour Fitness center (below), which opened in July 2007. (Above, courtesy Arcadia Public Library; below, Arcadia Historical Society.)

SANTA ANITA AVENUE LOOKING NORTH. This view of people walking north on the meandering, tree-lined track that was Santa Anita Avenue in the early years of the 20th century (left) clearly illustrates the rural feel of the city. This photograph was taken from the intersection of Orange Grove Boulevard and Santa Anita Avenue in 1916. Today the same area is home to the residential development known as the Highlands (below), and Santa Anita Avenue has become one of Arcadia's main arteries. (Left, courtesy Arcadia Public Library; below, Arcadia Historical Society.)

ARCADIA GARAGE/ARCADIA BODY SHOP. Located on the southeast corner of First Avenue and La Porte Street (above), the Arcadia Garage (also known as the A. W. Hibbard Building) also served as an auto repair shop and as city hall from June 1914 to April 1916. Prior to 1914, city hall was housed in Lucky Baldwin's Oakwood Hotel and the McCoy Building. Ninety years later, the Arcadia Body Shop (below) makes its home at the same location, and city hall has moved on to more appropriate and spacious accommodations. (Above, courtesy Arcadia Public Library; below, Arcadia Historical Society.)

A CENTURY OF UNION GAS. Though its name frequently changed, the station on the southwest corner of Foothill Boulevard and Santa Anita Avenue has been selling Union gas for more than 80 years. The station (above, around 1925) went by the name of White Oak Service Station, and owner Emil Bolz is pictured standing beside his two pumps. Inside he served everything from candy, peanuts, popcorn (5¢), ice cream, and cold drinks to cigars. Today the current Union 76 station (below) has more than 20 pumps. Snacks and cold drinks are still available (for more than 5¢), and awnings keep customers cool and dry. (Above, courtesy Arcadia Public Library; below, Arcadia Historical Society.)

ROSS FIELD/COUNTY PARK. The land now holding Los Angeles County's Arcadia Park and the Santa Anita Golf Course has undergone several transformations. Originally it was the site of Lucky Baldwin's first Thoroughbred racetrack. Then, in 1909, the State of California outlawed horse racing and the track was closed. In 1917, Anita Baldwin sold the land to the county, which deeded it to the War Department, which turned it into a school for training soldiers to operate hydrogen-filled balloons. This was Ross Field. The balloons were used for reconnaissance during World War I. In 1929, the Goodyear Blimp visited the balloon school (above), stopping near the hangars on the northwest side of what is now the golf course (below). (Above, courtesy Arcadia Public Library; below, Arcadia Historical Society.)

BALDWIN AVENUE BUSINESS DISTRICT. The 1000 block of Baldwin Avenue, located just south of Huntington Drive and north of the bowling alley, has been a thriving business district since the 1920s. Housing everything from an Asian art supply shop to a feed store, it has competed for business with the stores along Huntington Drive and First Avenue for over 80 years. Though many of the shops of the 1930s (above) are no longer in business, the area still looks remarkably similar today (below). One notable difference is the parking situation. Back in the 1930s, parking was on a diagonal. Today cars must either park parallel to the curb or they are prohibited. (Above, courtesy Arcadia Public Library; below, Arcadia Historical Society.)

EATON'S RESTAURANT, C. 1940. Located on the corner of Colorado Boulevard and Michillinda Avenue, Eaton's Santa Anita Restaurant and Motor Inn (above) was a favorite with hungry and tired patrons for 30 years—1939 to 1969. In this photograph, only the drive-in portion of the restaurant at 1130 West Colorado Boulevard is visible. Eaton's also offered traditional, in-house restaurant seating and motel accommodations. Shortly after Eaton's closed in September 1969, Coco's Restaurant (below) opened and has been thriving ever since. (Above, courtesy Arcadia Public Library; below, Arcadia Historical Society.)

RED CAR/AMTRAK/PULLMAN. Henry E. Huntington's popular Pacific Electric Railway system, better known as the Red Car Line, extended its service to Arcadia in 1903. The popular trains, which received power from overhead electrical lines, stopped at Lucky Baldwin's racetrack, the Ross Field balloon school during World War I, and Santa Anita Park when it was completed in 1934. Control towers, placed at intervals along the track (above), ensured the trains ran on time and that any problems were dealt with immediately. The one in this 1941 photograph was near First Avenue. Alternative transportation caused the demise of the Red Cars in 1951. The two privately owned rail cars (below), one a Pullman, are stored at roughly the same location—north of St. Joseph Street and just east of Santa Anita Avenue. (Above courtesy Arcadia Public Library; below, Arcadia Historical Society.)

CONTROL TOWER AND SELF-PROPELLED TRAIN. In 1885, the Santa Fe Railroad opened a line through Lucky Baldwin's ranch. A c. 1945 photograph (above) looks northwest along those tracks where an early version of a "self-propelled" rail car, control tower, and signal are visible near First Avenue and East Santa Clara Street. The cars ran from Los Angeles to San Bernardino. Santa Fe employees staffed the two control towers that oversaw the intersection of Santa Fe tracks with those of Pacific Electric Railway in Arcadia. Pacific Electric Railway service was shut down in 1951. Today the tracks and signal can still be seen on the southeast corner of First and Santa Clara Streets (below), and they may be used again if the Metro Gold Line is extended through Arcadia. (Above, courtesy Arcadia Public Library; below, Arcadia Historical Society.

HUNTINGTON DRIVE, MID-1940S/2007. As this 1940s photograph (above) eloquently illustrates, Huntington Drive has always been one of the busiest streets in Arcadia. Looking east from Santa Anita Avenue towards First Avenue, city hall and the busy commercial area are visible. City hall was still on the northwest corner of Huntington Drive and First Avenue at this point, and no attempts had been made to landscape the area. In the years that followed, trees, a decorative median, and left-turn lanes were added (below), and the tall streetlights were removed. Though shops such as the Arcadia Bootery and Seeley's Jewelry have long since disappeared, the spirit of entrepreneurship that has defined Arcadia from the start is still alive and well. (Above, courtesy Arcadia Public Library; below, Arcadia Historical Society.)

THE WESTERNER MOTEL, C. 1949. Built around 1947, the Westerner Motel at 161 Colorado Place was once a Best Western Motel (above). The motel's official name was Elite Westerner Inn and Suites, and it was a popular rest stop for visitors to Santa Anita Park, located directly across the street. Over time, business declined and the motel was demolished. The resulting empty lot (below), located just south of Peppers Mexican Grill and Cantina, has remained vacant ever since. (Above, courtesy Arcadia Public Library; below, Arcadia Historical Society)

CARL'S CORN STAND/RITE AID. One of Arcadia's most popular businesses during the 1940s and 1950s was Carl Kophamer's sweet corn stand (above), located at 75 West Las Tunas Drive, just west of Santa Anita Avenue. Opened in 1939, the stand was set up in front of a cornfield and sold fresh corn to passing travelers. By 1953, it was so popular that youngsters were competing for sales jobs as corn-girls and corn-boys. After the stand closed, the land became home to fast-food restaurants and office buildings. Today the area adjacent to the former stand has been developed into a retail strip mall (below). (Above, courtesy Arcadia Public Library; below, Arcadia Historical Society.)

FLAMINGO HOTEL/SANTA ANITA INN. The popular Pony Express Museum was dismantled in 1955 to make way for the Flamingo Hotel (above, around 1959 or 1960). Located at 130 West Huntington Drive, the hotel opened in 1956 and featured an A-frame lobby, an outdoor pool, cocktail lounge, café, children's playground, and live flamingos. The birds were kept near the driveway that led to the entrance to the hotel. In the same 6-acre location today is the Santa Anita Inn (below). The flamingos and A-frame lobby are long gone, replaced by groves of trees, flower gardens, walkways, and waterfalls. (Above, courtesy Arcadia Public Library; below, Arcadia Historical Society.)

HINSHAW'S/BURLINGTON COAT FACTORY. The first Hinshaw's department store opened in March 1952 on the southwest corner of Baldwin Avenue and Duarte Road. As the largest business in the area, it anchored the prosperous shopping complex for four decades before going out of business in 1992. Only the trees planted along the street by the city (above, around 1960) remain, and Burlington Coat Factory has taken over Hinshaw's space (below). The shopping center has also been remodeled. (Above, by Milton Bell of Monrovia, courtesy Arcadia Public Library; below, Arcadia Historical Society.)

BALDWIN RETAIL—EAST SIDE. In the 1960s, the east side of South Baldwin Avenue below Duarte Road was a varied and bustling block of businesses (above), including bakeries, barbershops, and men's and women's clothing stores. The arrival of the Santa Anita Fashion Park mall in 1976 (now known as Westfield Santa Anita) marked a decline in business, as competition from the mall was stiff. Many businesses have come and gone (below), and efforts have been made to give the area a face lift by planting trees and adding left-turn lanes. (Above, courtesy Arcadia Public Library; below, Arcadia Historical Society.)

FROM MUSTANGS TO MERCEDES. The north side of Huntington Drive—directly across from Los Angeles County's Arcadia Park and west of Santa Anita Avenue—has long been home to auto dealers. Huntington Ford (above, around 1966), located at 55 West Huntington Drive, rented and sold cars and trucks, including one of the earliest versions of the Mustang (priced at $3,000) and the Ranchero, a car/truck hybrid. Most recently, Paul Rusnak introduced the Rusnak Arcadia Mercedes-Benz dealership (below), selling luxury vehicles priced between $50,000 and $200,000. Rusnak has expanded operations east on Huntington Drive. (Above, by Milton Bell of Monrovia, courtesy Arcadia Public Library; below, Arcadia Historical Society.)

ARCADIA PUBLIC LIBRARY. Arcadia's first library was built on First Avenue and Wheeler Street in 1934. Within years, a larger facility was needed. Architect William Guy Garwood was engaged, and a new library was built on the southwest corner of Duarte Road and Santa Anita Avenue (above). The building featured a windowless facade and was dedicated in April 1961. The next major renovation occurred in 1996 when the library received a multimillion-dollar face lift and expansion. Architect Charles Walton and Associates designed the refurbishing, adding more than 12,000 square feet of space, computers, seating, facade, and entryway (below). (Above, courtesy Arcadia Public Library; below, Arcadia Historical Society.)

ARCADIA THEATERS. The primary movie theater for three decades in Arcadia was the Santa Anita Theater, also known as Edwards Santa Anita. Before it closed in the early 1970s, it became Cinemaland. It was demolished in 1977 (above). The theater opened in 1941, just a few years prior to the arrival of the Westerner Motel next door on Colorado Place (visible above at left). Arcadia's movie theaters are now confined to the Westfield Santa Anita Mall, where a 16-screen AMC complex was installed. The former site of the Santa Anita Theater is now occupied by the three-story Worley Parsons office building (below). (Above, courtesy Arcadia Public Library; below, Arcadia Historical Society.)

BIBLIOGRAPHY

Ainsworth, Ed. *Pot Luck: Episodes in the Life of W. Parker Lyon*. Hollywood, CA: George Palmer Putnam, Inc., 1940.

Bancroft, Hubert Howe. *Chronicles of the Builders of the Commonwealth, Volume III*. San Francisco: The History Company, 1892.

Eberly, Gordon S. *Arcadia—City of the Santa Anita*. Claremont, CA: Saunders Press, 1953.

Fleming, Mary, A. *History of the Thoroughbred in California*. Los Angeles: Sinclair Printing Company, 1983.

Glasscock, C. B. *Lucky Baldwin: The Story of an Unconventional Success*. Reno, NV: Silver Syndicate Press, 1993.

Hendrickson, Joe. *Tournament of Roses: The First 100 Years*. Los Angeles: The Knapp Press 1991.

McAdam, Pat and Sandy Snider. *Arcadia: Where Ranch and City Meet*. San Marino, CA: Golden West Books, 1981.

Snider, Sandra Lee. *Elias Jackson "Lucky" Baldwin, California Visionary*. Los Angeles: The Stairwell Group, 1987.

Visit us at
arcadiapublishing.com

....

www.ingramcontent.com/pod-product-compliance
Lightning Source LLC
Chambersburg PA
CBHW080549110426
42813CB00006B/1259